J 952 STE
Stefoff, Rebecca, 1951-
Japan

98070331

Vail Public Library
292 West Meadow Drive
Vail, CO   81657

‹ JAPAN ›

MAJOR WORLD NATIONS

JAPAN

Rebecca Stefoff

CHELSEA HOUSE PUBLISHERS
Philadelphia

VAIL PUBLIC LIBRARY

Chelsea House Publishers

Contributing Author: John Grabowski

Copyright © 1999 by Chelsea House Publishers,
a division of Main Line Book Co.
All rights reserved.
Printed and bound in the United States of America.

First Printing

1   3   5   7   9   8   6   4   2

Library of Congress Cataloging-in-Publication Data

Stefoff, Rebecca.
Japan.
Includes index.

Summary: An overview of the history, geography, economy,
government, people, and culture of Japan.

1. Japan. [1. Japan]
I. Title.
DS889.S655   1988   952.04   87-18322

ISBN 0-7910-4761-X
7   9   8   6

◄ C O N T E N T S ►

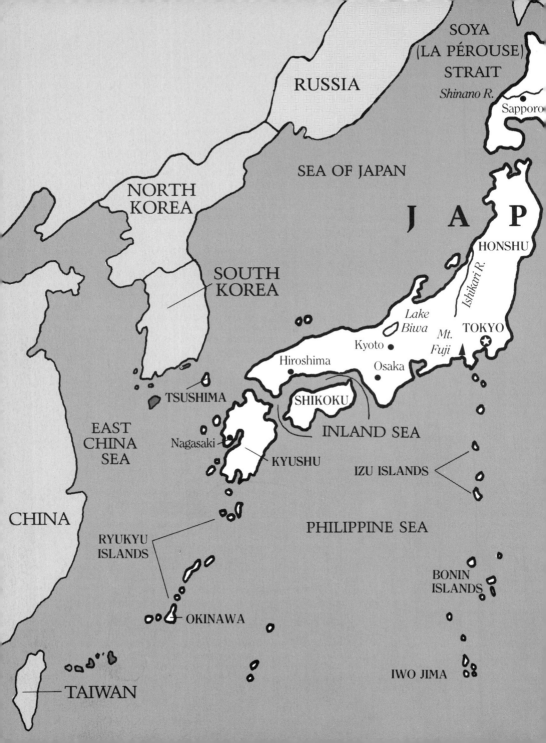

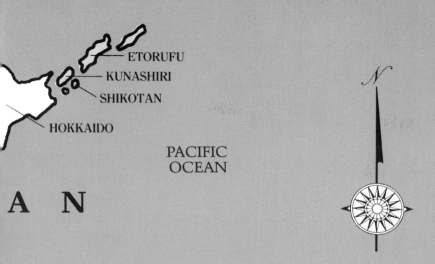

ETORUFU
KUNASHIRI
SHIKOTAN

HOKKAIDO

PACIFIC
OCEAN

A N

N

RUSSIA

MONGOLIA

NORTH
KOREA

PACIFIC OCEAN

CHINA

SOUTH
KOREA

J A P A N

TAIWAN

◄ FACTS AT A GLANCE ►

Land and People

Area	145,862 square miles (377,781 square kilometers)
Highest Point	Mount Fuji, 12,388 feet (3,776 meters)
Capital	Tokyo (population 7,962,000)
Other Major Cities	Yokohama (population 3,320,000), Osaka (population 2,600,000), Nagoya (population 2,151,000), Sapporo (population 1,774,000), Kyoto (population 1,464,000)
Population	125,612,000
Population Density	861 people per square mile (332 per sq km)
Population Distribution	Urban, 77.6 percent; rural, 22.4 percent
Language	Japanese
Ethnic Groups	Japanese, 98.9 percent; Korean, 0.5 percent; other, 0.6 percent
Religions	Shintoist, 95 percent; Buddhist, 72 percent (most Japanese practice both Shinto and Buddhism); Christian, 1 percent
Literacy Rate	100 percent
Average Life Expectancy	Males, 77 years; females, 83 years
Infant Mortality Rate	4.4 deaths per 1,000 live births

Economy

Major Resources	Fish, timber
Major Products	Automobiles, electronic equipment, textiles, rice, chemicals, steel, machinery
Employment	Services, 36.9 percent; trade, manufacturing, mining, and construction, 54.2 percent; agriculture and fishing, 5.6 percent; government, 3.2 percent
Currency	Yen (approximately 112 yen equal U.S. $1)

Government

Form of Government	Parliamentary democracy, with two legislative houses (together called the Diet) and a cabinet of ministers
Subdivisions	Prefectures administered by governors and assemblies
Formal Head of State	Emperor, hereditary monarch
Head of Government	Prime minister, elected by the Diet and formally appointed by the emperor
Eligibility to Vote	All men and women over 20 years old may vote for legislators, governors, municipal mayors, and assembly members

◄HISTORY AT A GLANCE►

30,000 to 10,000 B.C.	The settlement of Japan begins. The islands are linked to mainland Asia by land bridges.
5000 to 300 B.C.	Hunter-gatherers called the Jomon people form small settlements. The Jomon are known for their decorated pottery.
300 B.C.	The Yayoi culture replaces the Jomon culture and introduces irrigated rice cultivation and metalworking from Korea.
about 400 A.D.	The Yamato clan of southern Honshu rises to power. The Yamato rulers encourage cultural exchange and trade with China.
405	Japan accepts Chinese characters as its official written language.
538 to 552	Buddhism and Confucianism enter from Korea.
604	Prince Shotoku issues Japan's first constitution. Japan sends its first ambassador to China.
645	The Taika Reform models the Yamato government on the Chinese system. The emperor introduces taxes and a legal system.
710	The imperial court moves to the new capital city of Nara. Buddhism flourishes.
712	The *Kojiki* (Japan's first written history) and *The Collection of Ten Thousand Leaves* (its first poetry anthology) are written.
794	The imperial capital moves from Nara to Heian (present-day Kyoto).

858	The Fujiwara family rises to power as ministers and regents to several emperors.
about 1000	Courtiers refine the classic Japanese arts of calligraphy, flower arranging, and poetry. Lady Murasaki Shikibu writes *The Tale of Genji*, the world's first novel.
about 1150	The warrior class (samurai) emerges to manage affairs in the provinces. The samurai grow powerful and struggle for control of the court.
1160 to 1180	The Taira family controls the court.
1185	After five years of war, the Minamoto family overcomes the Taira and sets up a military government.
1191	Zen Buddhism is introduced from China. Zen priests begin drinking tea as an aid to meditation. It soon becomes the national drink.
1192	The emperor names Minamoto Yoritomo the first shogun (military ruler). Kamakura, south of modern Tokyo, gradually becomes the center of shogun government.
1274 and 1281	The Mongol Empire under Kublai Khan twice tries to invade Japan. Storms sink both Mongol fleets. The Japanese call the storms *kamikaze* (divine winds).
1336	General Ashikaga overthrows the Kamakura shogunate and establishes his own dynasty, with Kyoto as its capital.
1397	The Golden Pavilion is built in Kyoto.
1467 to 1477	The Onin War (civil war) devastates Kyoto.
1543	Portuguese traders arrive and introduce Western guns, commerce, and Christianity.
1549	St. Francis Xavier establishes a Jesuit mission in Japan.

1560 to 1590	Military leaders Oda Nobunaga and Toyotomi Hideyoshi unify the country.
1582	Ambassadors from authorities in Kyushu reach the pope in Rome. Many provincial Japanese have become Christians.
1592 to 1598	Hideyoshi tries unsuccessfully to conquer Korea. He dies in 1598.
1603	Tokugawa Ieyasu founds the Tokugawa shogunate, which will rule Japan for 250 years. He moves the capital to Edo (modern Tokyo).
1609	Dutch merchants receive permission to trade in Japan.
about 1640	The shogunate closes off Japan from the rest of the world. Christian missionaries are expelled. Japanese citizens may not leave the country, and only Dutch and Chinese traders are allowed to enter Nagasaki, the country's trade port.
1720	The ban on foreign books is lifted. Scholars study Dutch works on science and medicine.
1796	The first Japanese dictionary (which translates Japanese to Dutch) is completed.
1853	Commodore Matthew C. Perry sails into Tokyo Bay to force Japan to grant trading rights to the United States.
1854	Perry returns and signs a treaty with the shogun.
1856	Townsend Harris becomes the first U.S. consul in Japan. Diplomatic and trade relations with the Netherlands, Russia, France, and Great Britain soon follow.
1867	The Emperor Meiji, backed by young samurai, overthrows the Tokugawa shogunate. He introduces widespread reforms and sets out to mod-

ernize Japan and abolish the samurai.

1877 The last great samurai revolt against the Meiji Restoration fails.

1885 to 1890 A prime minister and cabinet are appointed, a constitution is written, and the first parliamentary elections are held.

1894 to 1895 Japan and China go to war. Japan wins some overseas territory.

1904 to 1905 Japan and Russia go to war. Japan wins more territory on the Asian mainland.

1926 Emperor Hirohito ascends the throne.

1931 Japan invades Manchuria.

1937 Japan wages war with China on the mainland.

1941 Japan comes under military rule after General Tojo Hideki names himself prime minister and supreme military commander. On December 7, Japan attacks the United States fleet at Pearl Harbor, Hawaii. The next day, the U.S. declares war on Japan and both nations enter World War II.

1942 Japan experiences its first major defeat of the war at the Battle of Midway in June.

1944 United States bombers come within range of Tokyo.

1945 The United States launches massive bombing raids on major Japanese cities. General Tojo's government is deposed. In August, the U.S. drops atomic bombs on Hiroshima and Nagasaki. Japan surrenders.

1945 to 1952 Under the command of United States General Douglas MacArthur, Allied forces occupy Japan. MacArthur requires Emperor Hirohito to state publicly that he is not a god. The Allies institute widespread political, economic, and social reforms, including granting women the right to vote.

1952	Japan's sovereignty is officially restored.
1968, 1972	United States returns to Japan several island groups seized during World War II, including Okinawa. But some U.S. troops continue to be stationed on Okinawa.
early 1980s	Japan's resurgent economy earns recognition as a major competitor for the United States and western Europe.
1989	Emperor Hirohito dies and is succeeded by his son Akihito.
1993	Crown Prince Naruhito marries a commoner, Owada Masako.
January 1995	Earthquake strikes near Kobe, resulting in more than 4,000 deaths.
March 1995	Poisonous nerve gas attacks in Tokyo subway system, attributed to a small religious cult, leave 12 dead and more than 5,500 injured.
1996	After a scandal involving U.S. servicemen, the United States agrees to begin phasing out its military presence on Okinawa.
1998	Winter Olympics are held at Nagano.

Until the 1800s, Westerners knew little about the ancient Japanese empire and its legendary rulers, such as the 8th-century emperor Kammu.

Japan and the World

For hundreds of years, the island nation of Japan—called Nihon or Nippon (Land of the Rising Sun) by its inhabitants—was a remote and isolated land. Generations of feudal rulers kept the country cut off from most other nations and cultures until the 19th century. Although Japanese culture had flourished for thousands of years, the rest of the world knew virtually nothing about Japan and its people until it opened its doors to the West in 1854.

Today, Japan has considerably expanded its role in world affairs. During the 20th century, it has changed from a remote, underdeveloped country into a modern nation of great international importance. It is a leading economic power, second only to the United States in its yearly production of goods and services. It is one of the world's foremost shipbuilders and a major producer of steel, automobiles, and manufactured items. Overall, Japan has one of the world's strongest industrial economies.

Japan's industrial success is especially remarkable because it occurred so rapidly. Until the late 19th century, the country had a rural economy. Most people lived in small villages and either farmed or practiced handicrafts. But after Japan was opened to trade with the rest of the world in 1854, its small harbor towns grew into large,

The Japanese are one of the world's best-educated peoples.

thriving port cities. Emperor Meiji, who took the throne in 1868, worked to bring Japan quickly into the modern world by making education widely available, urging people to study Western customs and ways of life, and promoting the growth of factories modeled on those of the United States and Europe.

But it was only after World War II, when most of the country lay in ruins, that Japan leaped into the economic limelight. In just a few decades, it rebuilt its cities and harbors, created the world's most modern and efficient transportation system, constructed thousands of new factories (many of them now operated by robots and remote-controlled machinery), and began to sell millions of dollars' worth of high-quality, high-technology goods to other nations.

Today, Japan is an economic and industrial leader, and Japanese brand names are familiar to consumers everywhere. Corporations in the United States and other countries have studied Japanese business methods, hoping to equal Japanese productivity. And because of its prosperous international trade, Japan's standard of living is one of the highest in the world.

Japan's importance to the world stems from noneconomic factors as well. During World War II, the United States dropped the only atomic bombs ever used in war on the Japanese port cities of Hiroshima and Nagasaki. Scientists are now studying the long-term effects of atomic radiation on Japan's people, plants, and animals. Having survived two nuclear attacks and seen the devastation they caused, the Japanese have decided never to develop nuclear weapons or to sell arms to other nations.

Japan's international presence is growing in other ways, too. Japan is now the world's largest donor of aid to foreign nations, providing nearly $15 billion in annual aid by the mid-1990s. The country also plays a leading role in several associations of Asian and Pacific nations. Japan's leadership in Asia is especially important because many scholars and political scientists believe that the 21st century will become the Asian-Pacific era, when the nations of the Pacific Ocean and Asia take on major international importance. Thus the once-isolated country of Japan is poised to be at the forefront of world affairs in the years to come.

Japan is a land of incredible natural beauty, and it has been made even more beautiful through the art of landscaping, which many Japanese practice.

The Land

Japan is noted all over the world for the beauty and variety of its *sansui*, or landscape. The country's diverse scenery includes coral reefs, snowy mountain peaks crowded with skiers, quiet islands wreathed in mist, northern evergreen forests, balmy beaches, and carefully cultivated terraces and rice paddies, all crowded—sometimes within only a few miles (kilometers) of each other—into a land slightly smaller than the state of California.

The 4 large and 3,000 or more small islands that make up Japan lie in the northern Pacific Ocean, off the east coast of Asia. Together, they cover a land area of 145,862 square miles (377,781 square kilometers) and extend about 1,730 miles (2,785 km) from north to south. The largest island is Honshu. Long, thin, and crescent-shaped, it contains most of Japan's people and cities, including the capital, Tokyo. The second largest island is Hokkaido, north of Honshu. It is sparsely populated. Kyushu, the southernmost of the four large islands, is the third largest and second most densely populated. Shikoku, the smallest and least populated of the large islands, lies just to the east of southern Honshu and to the north of Kyushu.

Two chains of small islands reaching out from the larger ones also belong to Japan. One of these chains consists of the Izu and

Bonin islands, scattered in a line that points south from the center of Honshu's eastern coast near Tokyo. At the southern end of the Bonin Islands is the tiny isle of Iwo Jima, the site of a famous World War II battle. The other island chain stretches southwest from the southern tip of Kyushu. Called the Ryukyu Islands, it includes the island of Okinawa, also the scene of fighting during World War II.

Most of the Ryukyu, Izo, and Bonin islands are volcanic peaks, steep and craggy. Some, however, are low, flat coral islands, formed by the tiny coral polyps that thrive in the warmer waters south of the main islands. These subtropical islands, complete with white sand beaches, palm trees, and flaming sunsets, have become favored vacation and honeymoon spots for the Japanese.

In addition to these island groups, Japan includes as many as 3,000 small islands scattered along the coasts of the larger ones. Some of these tiny islands have names and inhabitants; others are only rocks, barren or covered with low, wind-twisted pine trees.

Japan's neighbor to the north is Russia. Russia's Sakhalin Peninsula is only 10 miles (16 kilometers) from the northern tip of Hokkaido, across a stretch of sea called the Soya (or La Pérouse) Strait. The three small islands of Kunashiri, Etorufu, and Shikotan, just off Hokkaido's northeastern shore, are now administered by Russia, although Japan still claims them.

Many of Japan's snow-capped mountain peaks have become popular skiing areas.

To the west, Japan is bordered by the Sea of Japan. Although this sea is small, it is quite deep, measuring 12,276 feet (3,683 meters) at its deepest point. On the other side of the Sea of Japan lie Russia and North and South Korea. To the southwest, the broad, shallow East China Sea separates Japan from the People's Republic of China. The Philippine Sea forms the islands' southern border. To the southeast and east lies the North Pacific Ocean. Just east of the islands is one of the world's deepest ocean-floor trenches, more than 26,000 feet (7,800 m) deep.

In the waters around Japan, cold currents from the north meet warm currents from the tropical south. The biggest such current is the Kuroshio, sometimes called the Japan Current or the Black Stream. Like the Gulf Stream in the Atlantic Ocean, it carries warm water into northerly latitudes. Where the warm water meets colder water or cold air, it produces fog and rain. Because of the Kuroshio and other currents, Japan's weather is cool and damp.

Another important body of water is the Inland Sea (called the Seto Naikai in Japanese). A 300-mile- (483-kilometer-) long waterway that runs between Honshu on the north and Shikoku and Kyushu on the south, the Inland Sea is connected to the Pacific by the Kii and Bungo straits in the east and to the Sea of Japan by the narrow Shimonoseki Strait in the west. Its calm, easily navigated waters are dotted with several thousand small islands, some of which house picturesque fishing villages or ancient religious shrines. The water's rugged coastline, craggy with rocks and cliffs, is indented with hundreds of bays and coves. Early Japanese civilization flourished in the cities and plains along the Inland Sea, and today, some of the country's largest industrial centers are found along its northern shores. But large areas of the Inland Sea have been set aside as a national park to preserve their natural beauty.

Much of Japan's coastline resembles that of the Inland Sea. Its many indentations and promontories make the coast much longer than it appears: the country has 9 miles of coastline for every square mile of territory (23 kilometers per square kilometer). No part of Japan is more than 75 miles (121 km) from the sea, and the water has long played a major role in the economy and way of life of the Japanese people.

Japan is also a land of mountains and volcanoes. The Japanese islands are actually an archipelago, or a chain of submerged mountains. These immense peaks sank beneath the sea eons ago; today, only their peaks and upper slopes remain above the water. Traces of the seismic activity that probably caused them to sink remain in the many volcanoes of the islands. Of Japan's more than 150 major volcanoes, at least 60 have erupted in recorded history.

The Odaki Waterfall sits in the shadow of Japan's highest point, Mt. Fuji.

Mount Aso, in Kyushu, has one of the largest calderas (volcanic craters) in the world, measuring 71 miles (114 kilometers) around. The dormant volcanic peak Mount Fuji (called Fujiyama by the Japanese) is the highest point in Japan, rising to 12,388 feet (3,776 meters) above sea level. Its perfect conical shape, dark blue at the base and topped with sparkling white snow, is one of the loveliest sights in the islands and is known all over the world. Deep lakes, such as Kutcharo, Towada, and Ashi, have formed in the craters of other, extinct volcanoes.

Japan's volcanic activity also appears in the forms of hot springs and earthquakes. Thousands of hot springs are scattered throughout the islands, and many of them have been known for centuries as health and pleasure resorts. Japan averages four earthquakes a day. Most of them are tiny tremors that can hardly be felt, but some are larger, causing houses to sway and dishes to fall off shelves. The Japanese are skilled at building everything—from traditional wooden houses to modern steel-and-glass skyscrapers—to move gently with the earth's tremors rather than splitting. Yet, once in about every six years, massive earthquakes do fearful damage, especially in the crowded cities. The most severe quakes of recent years have been in Honshu and Hokkaido.

The major elements of Japan's topography are volcanoes and short, steep mountain ranges that sometimes meet in clusters of peaks. The Kitami, Teshio, and Kidaka are the chief ranges of the island of Hokkaido, and Shikoku and Kyushu both have ranges that bear the same names as the islands.

The island of Honshu has numerous mountain ranges, most of which run roughly north-to-south. The Ou, Echigo, Kitakami, and Abukama are the chief ranges in the north. In the center of the island rise three parallel mountain chains—the Hida (or Northern) Alps, the Kizo (Central) Alps, and the Akaishi (Southern) Alps—that together are called the Japan Alps. Their highest peak is Kitadake, in the Southern Alps, which reaches 10,474 feet (3,192 meters). Mount Fuji, which is not part of the Japan Alps, is about 35 miles (56 kilometers) south of the Southern Alps, and Tokyo is 125 miles (201 km) east of them. The Kii and Chugoku ranges run through the southern and western portions of Honshu.

All told, these rugged mountain chains account for nearly 85 percent of Japan's land area; only about 15 percent is level enough for farming or building. The largest flatland area is the Kanto Plain, which covers about 5,000 square miles (13,100 square kilometers) on the eastern coast of Honshu north of Tokyo. This plain and many other, smaller, coastal lowlands (called *heiya*) make up the country's principal areas of agriculture and settlement.

Many lakes are scattered among the plains and mountains. The largest is Lake Biwa, in central western Honshu, which covers 260 square miles (681 square kilometers). Most of the lakes are much smaller. Some of them have scenic or recreational value; others support local fishing industries.

Mountains cover most of Japan's surface, leaving little land for farming.

Nearly all of Japan's more than 100 rivers are short and swift. They are useless for navigation, and because of the difficulty of building dams in the mountainous terrain, they do not provide much hydroelectric power. The longest rivers are: the 229-mile (369-kilometer) Shinano, in northwest Honshu; the 227-mile (365-km) Ishikari, in western Hokkaido; and the Tone, which runs for 200 miles (320 km) through the Kanto Plain.

Climate and Rainfall

Japan covers approximately the same latitude as North America between Montreal and the Gulf of Mexico. Therefore, the two areas have similarly wide-ranging climates. Hokkaido, in the north, is snowy and quite cold in the winter and cool, damp, and foggy in the summer. Northern Honshu is similar to Hokkaido, but its central and western regions have a more moderate climate, with warmer summers. Southern Shikoku and southern Kyushu are milder still, and the subtropical island chains to the south are humid and warm all year round.

The eastern, or Pacific, coasts of the islands have somewhat different weather than the western, or Sea of Japan, coasts. In the east, winter weather is likely to be bright and windy, while winters on the west coast are cloudy, snowy, or rainy. Destructive typhoons (storms, similar to hurricanes, that arise at sea and bring high winds and rising waters) sometimes strike the coast during the summer and early fall, especially in the southwest.

Temperatures in Hokkaido range from 16° Fahrenheit ($-9°$ Centigrade) in January to 70° F (21° C) in August. In Tokyo, January temperatures average 39° F (4° C) and August temperatures average 81° F (27° C). Okinawa, in the southern Ryukyus, is about 15° F (6.5° C) warmer year round. Throughout the country, inland temperatures are cooler than those of the seacoasts, and the temperature drops as the altitude increases in mountainous areas.

Japan's average annual rainfall is 70 inches (1,778 millimeters), and most parts of the country receive at least 40 inches (1,016 mm) of precipitation each year. The driest place is eastern Hokkaido, which receives about 37 inches (940 mm) of rain yearly. The wettest area, the Kii Peninsula of central Honshu, gets more than 160 inches (4,064 mm).

Early summer is the rainiest time of year, and the heaviest rains fall in June; they are called *baiu*, or "plum rains," because they begin when the plums are ripening on the trees. Snowfall in Japan varies as much as rainfall. It is heaviest in Hokkaido, in northern and inland Honshu, and on the northwest coast of Honshu along the Sea of Japan. These regions are covered with snow from November to April.

Plant and Animal Life

Japan's plants and animals are as varied as its landscape and climate. Many species of plants and animals are the same as those found throughout the Asian continent and in North America. A few species, however, thrive only in Japan.

Because so much of Japan is mountainous and unsuitable for farming, many areas have never been cleared and remain heavily forested. Evergreens such as spruce and fir trees grow in Hokkaido, as do birches, oaks, and maples. The same trees also thrive in the higher altitudes of Honshu, mixed with graceful stands of tall bamboo plants. Along the coastlines of southern Honshu, Kyushu, and Shikoku, fig trees and fan palms grow among pines in the sandy dunes. Camphor bushes also are found in the coastal lowlands. Mangrove swamps—marshy areas of low, twisted trees that grow on tidal flats—cover some parts of southern Kyushu. On Yaku-shima, an island between Kyushu and the Ryukyu Islands, rise stands of Japanese cedar with trees more than 2,000 years old.

Japan's human inhabitants have greatly changed its natural vegetation over the centuries. They introduced many plants—peach

The Japanese are avid landscapers. Many gardens are carefully crafted works of art.

and plum trees, melons, and especially rice—from China, for agricultural purposes. In the southern islands, they planted mulberry trees, the home and food of the silkworms that produce fine silk.

The Japanese have further altered the vegetation of their islands through their national passion for landscape gardening. They prize trees such as maple, beech, oak, and birch for their colorful autumn leaves and have planted them in groves in many parts of Japan, even in remote and unpopulated regions. Larches, cedars, red and black pines, and other species have also been introduced into some regions to enhance the beauty of the landscape. And cherry trees, beloved by the Japanese for their pink-and-white spring blossoms, now grow everywhere, although they originally occurred naturally only in some mountain ranges. Many Japanese also cultivate flowers and flowering shrubs, especially irises, chrysanthemums, and azaleas.

Because most of Japan's people are concentrated in the coastal regions, large areas of the islands, especially in the mountainous interiors, are sparsely inhabited. As a result, Japan's wildlife continues to flourish in these regions. Bears, wolves, and wild boar survive there, along with foxes, deer, antelope, mink, weasels, badgers, and *tanuki*—wild dogs found only in Japan and sometimes called raccoon dogs because of their masklike coloring. Japan's one native species of monkey, the Japanese macaque, lives farther north than any other monkey species; its habitat stretches to northern Honshu.

The 450 species of birds in Japan include sea birds (gulls, terns, and auks), songbirds (larks and finches), water birds (storks, ducks, geese, and herons), and birds of prey (eagles and hawks). The cormorant, a diving bird, can be trained to aid fishermen by diving for and retrieving fish; the birds are prevented from swallowing their prey by metal rings around their necks. Another bird, the *toki*, or Japanese crested ibis, often appears in old drawings and paintings. The toki was once common but is now almost extinct.

About 30 species of reptiles inhabit Japan, including tortoises, sea turtles, and two varieties of poisonous snake (both very rare). The largest snake, the Japanese rat snake, grows to 6 feet (2 meters) in length but is harmless. In the mountain streams of Kyushu and western Honshu lives the rare Japanese giant salamander. About 5 feet (1.5 m) long, it is one of the largest amphibian species in the world.

The seas around Japan teem with life, including whales, seals, porpoises, mackerel, sea bream, tuna, herring, mullet, cod, crabs, shrimp, clams, and oysters. Trout, salmon, and crayfish swim in the rivers and streams. The Japanese have a long tradition of fishing, and seafood is an important part of the national diet. They cultivate oysters, clams, and several varieties of seaweed on underwater farms; this sea life is a source of food and—in the case of the oysters—pearls.

Many species of insects thrive in Japan, including the Japanese beetle. This insect is also found in North America and Europe, where it is shiny, greenish purple in color, and causes much damage to trees. In its native country, it is a dull brown and is kept in check by natural enemies. Butterflies, moths, bees, wasps, mosquitoes, and spiders are common. Fireflies and crickets are numerous during the summer, and many Japanese catch and keep them in small wooden or bamboo cages for good luck.

Japan is a land of long-standing traditions. Emperor Hirohito (1901–89), shown here in traditional dress, was descended from several centuries of emperors.

An Island Empire

During Japan's Stone Age, from 30,000 to 10,000 B.C., the world's oceans were shallower than they are today, and the Japanese islands were connected to the Asian continent by several narrow land bridges. Japan's earliest known inhabitants migrated across these bridges from Korea and northern Asia. The early island-dwellers were probably hunter-gatherers (wandering family groups who lived by hunting and by finding wild grains and vegetables, rather than by farming). They used fire and stone tools, and they lived in caves or in cavelike pits dug into the ground.

In about 5000 B.C., these primitive people began to gather in larger groups and to form a more advanced civilization. They discovered how to sculpt clay pottery, which they decorated with patterns made by knotted cords. Because of this skill, their civilization is today called the Jomon culture, from the Japanese word *jomon*, which means "cord marks." Many pieces of their distinctive pottery have been found throughout Japan and are on display in museums.

The Jomon civilization lasted until about 300 B.C., when a new culture arose in Kyushu and quickly spread to other islands. Called the Yayoi (after a suburb in Tokyo where its relics were first dug up in 1884), this new group practiced pottery-making on potter's wheels, metalworking, and rice growing—skills most likely learned from the southern Chinese or Koreans, who had mastered them several centuries earlier. The Yayoi people also buried their dead in mounds of earth, which were sometimes marked with huge standing stones. Swords, beads, and mirrors were buried along with the dead in these graves.

The Yayoi civilization lasted for five or six centuries, during which social groups and settlements grew larger as the basic unit of society shifted from the family to the clan (a cluster of families related by blood or marriage). One such clan, the Yamato of southern Honshu, grew steadily more powerful after about 300 A.D.

During the same period, clans throughout Japan started building immense burial mounds for their dead chiefs. This tradition lasted for 350 years, and by the end of the 7th century, more than 20,000 mounds had been built. Some of them are among the largest grave mounds in the world. Many contain bronze sculptures, called *haniwa*, that may have represented the dead men's horses and warriors.

By 400, the Yamato clan was the most powerful in Japan. The other clans pledged their loyalty, and the Yamato received trade and diplomatic envoys from the imperial court of China and waged war on some of the small kingdoms of the Korean peninsula. The Yamato leaders claimed to be descended from the sun goddess, Amaterasu. Sometime in the 5th century, one of them took the title of *tenno*, or "emperor of heaven." The imperial line founded long ago by this chieftain has never been broken; Akihito, who occupies the emperor's throne today, is one of his descendants.

Toward the end of the 6th century, some Japanese clans began to waver in their allegiance to the Yamato. A few even plotted with the rulers of Korean states against the emperor. As a result, the Yamato court lost power both abroad and at home. Before it fell into decline, however, an event of tremendous importance in Japan's

Prince Shotoku issued Japan's first constitution and strengthened Yamato rule.

history took place: the religion of Buddhism was introduced from the Korean kingdom of Paekche. By 552, it had been adopted as the official religion of the Yamato court.

This exotic new belief, which held that self-purification would relieve suffering, spread quickly through the islands and grew to have a tremendous influence on Japanese culture. In most cases, it mixed comfortably with the native religion of Shinto, which consisted of reverence for ancestors, belief in local gods and spirits, and preservation of folklore and ritual. Confucianism, a Chinese system of philosophical principles to guide correct behavior, also spread through Japan and mixed with Buddhism and Shinto.

In 604, the young Prince Shotoku took charge of the country on behalf of his aunt, the empress, and brought new strength to the Yamato rule. He issued Japan's first constitution, which placed the emperor at the head of the state and outlined his subjects' ranks and duties. It became the basic law of the nation. Shotoku also devoted himself to the study of Buddhism and built many temples. One of them, called Horyuji, was founded in 607 near the present-day city of Nara. Its original structure still stands. It is Japan's oldest temple and the world's oldest surviving wooden building.

After Shotoku's death in 629, the powerful Soga family tried to take over the remnants of the Yamato empire. In 645, however, the Soga were overthrown and a Yamato tenno reclaimed the throne. In 646, the Yamato introduced the Taika Reform, which reorganized the imperial government on the Chinese model by instituting taxes, a legal system, and a division of the country into administrative provinces. The imperial capital was moved to Nara in 710. For nearly a century, this new city was the seat of government and also a flourishing center of Buddhist study and worship.

In 794, the emperor Kammu began constructing a new capital city, called Heian, on the site of present-day Kyoto. Modeled on the ancient Chinese capital of Changan, it was laid out in a checkerboard pattern and contained hundreds of temples, shrines, and palaces. Heian remained the official capital of Japan for more than 1,000 years, even when the true seat of power sometimes shifted elsewhere for brief periods.

Although the imperial line remained unbroken, the emperor's power waned after about 850, when a nine-year-old prince ascended the throne. Regents (officials who rule for an emperor who is unable to govern effectively because of age or illness) and councillors gradually seized control of the government. The Fujiwara clan married into the imperial family for several generations in a row and monopolized high government posts. The Yamato emperors continued to be worshipped as gods but they no longer had real political power.

As the Fujiwara grew wealthy and powerful, a new force arose in the outlying provinces of the empire. This new force was the warrior class of the *samurai,* who began as administrators of the provinces and villages but quickly took on the role of military police in the cities. There, they associated with the Fujiwara and other noble clans and acquired a foothold at court. The two most powerful samurai clans were the Minamoto and the Taira; both were descended from emperors. The samurai lived by a rigorous code of behavior called *bushido,* or "the way of the warrior," which stressed honor and courage above all other virtues. Samurai who did not live up to the standards of bushido were expected to kill themselves by disembowelment in a ceremony called *hara-kiri.*

For a time, the Japanese government ran smoothly, with the emperors studying Buddhism or writing poetry in the lavish palace at Heian, the Fujiwara and other noble clans managing the country's affairs, and the samurai collecting taxes and keeping order throughout the land. In about 1150, however, the samurai grew hungry for greater power, and the Taira and Minamoto clans began a struggle to take over the government. The Taira emerged victorious and went on to rule the court from 1160 to 1180. The Minamoto vowed revenge, and after a bitter five-year war they seized power in 1185 with the help of the Fujiwara clan. After wiping out the fleeing Taira in a sea battle off the coast of Shikoku, they picked up the reins of rulership.

At this point, the structure of the Japanese government underwent a profound and long-lasting change. The head of the victorious clan, Minamoto Yoritomo (in traditional Japanese names, the personal name follows the family name), gave himself the title of shogun, or "military ruler." The emperor confirmed the title in 1192— probably under duress. Because the shogun also had the support of most of the warriors, he became the most powerful man in the empire. He ran the country from his headquarters in Kamakura, about 30 miles (48 kilometers) from modern Tokyo, while the emperor was allowed to maintain the appearance of royalty in the court at Heian. This form of military government was known as a shogunate or, in Japanese, as *bakufu* ("tent government," or government from the field of battle). Japan was ruled by a series of shogunates for nearly 700 years.

Under the Shoguns

During his reign, Yoritomo killed most of his relatives, fearing that they would try to usurp his power. After his death in 1199, another clan, the Hojo (related to Yoritomo's wife), selected shoguns from the Fujiwara and other strong clans to head a new Kamakura shogunate. Under these shoguns, the samurai of Japan adopted the new sect of Zen Buddhism (the belief that enlightenment could be attained through meditation) that had entered the islands from China.

Not everything that came from the Chinese mainland was welcomed in Japan, however. In the 13th century, China was ruled by Kublai Khan, emperor of the Mongols and grandson of Genghis Khan, who had conquered most of east central Asia in the early 13th century. In 1259, Kublai Khan conquered Korea and ordered Japan to submit to his authority. The warriors of Kamakura responded by cutting off the heads of his ambassadors.

A great statue of Buddha stands at Kamakura, site of a powerful 12th-century shogunate.

In 1274, the khan sent a mighty fleet across the Sea of Japan. It landed on the west coast of Kyushu but was forced to retreat by a typhoon. Still determined to possess Japan, the khan sent an even larger invasion fleet—150,000 men—in 1281. These ships landed on Kyushu but were almost immediately destroyed by another violent typhoon. The few Mongol soldiers who survived the storm were slain by the samurai warriors. The Japanese named the two storms that had saved them from invasion *kamikaze* (divine winds). Much later, during World War II, Japanese airmen were called kamikaze fighters, in honor of these 13th-century typhoons.

The Kamakura shogunate ruled Japan until 1331, when the emperor Godaigo led a revolt. Although the revolt succeeded, Godaigo did not gain control of the country. Instead, one of his generals, Ashikaga, turned against him, had himself named shogun and set one of Godaigo's relatives on the imperial throne. Godaigo set up a rival court in the mountains south of Nara. He and his descendants resisted the Ashikaga shogunate for 60 years but were unable to regain any power. They finally died out.

The Ashikaga shogunate ruled Japan until 1573. The Ashikaga were patrons of the arts, so painting, flower arranging, and other Japanese art forms flourished during this period. Trade and craftsmanship also thrived. One powerful shogun, Ashikaga Yoshimitsu, built a splendid Zen Buddhist temple in Kyoto called the Golden Pavilion. It was one of Japan's most important shrines until 1950, when it was destroyed by an arsonist. (It was rebuilt in 1955.)

The Ashikaga were weak rulers, and rebellions sprang up in many parts of the empire. In 1467, civil war broke out in Kyoto over the question of succession to the shogunate. Rival groups within the Ashikaga clan joined with other clans and fought in and around the capital city for a decade, reducing many of its fine buildings to rubble in a civil war that later became known as the Onin War. After a few years, the rebellion spread to the provinces, and provincial samurai administrators began to set themselves up as *daimyo* (domain lords), or rulers of estates or regions. The daimyo became increasingly powerful in Japanese politics.

For a century after the Onin War, a series of weak shoguns strove to reunite the empire, but powerful daimyo resisted their control. Some daimyo issued their own laws and constitutions. Fighting and unrest plagued the islands. Much havoc was caused by the *ronin* (masterless samurai), wandering warriors who would fight for anyone who paid them and who often set up as bandits or highway robbers. This troubled time in Japan's history is now known as the "Warring Country" period.

In 1543, when the Warring Country was at the peak of its strife, a new element entered Japanese history. The isolated island empire had its first contact with the Western world.

East Meets West

The first meeting between the East and the West in Japan was far from glorious. Three Portuguese sailors were shipwrecked and washed ashore on Tanega Shima, a small island off the southeastern coast of Kyushu. These luckless mariners were taken in by a local daimyo. In return for his hospitality, they taught him how to make European-style muskets. The new art of making and using firearms spread quickly throughout Japan and fueled its civil strife.

The Portuguese and Spanish had been venturing into Asia ever since Vasco da Gama had sailed around Africa to India in the early 16th century. By the middle of the century, the two nations had explored all but the most remote coasts and islands of the continent and were moving north through the East China and Philippine seas. The Dutch were not far behind them.

In the wake of the first explorers and traders to enter these new regions came the missionary movement. In 1549, the Jesuit missionary Francis Xavier (later Saint Francis Xavier) arrived in Japan.

He established a Jesuit mission in Kagoshima, on Kyushu, and ran it for two years, converting many Japanese to Catholicism. By 1580, there were 150,000 Christian converts in Japan, and by the early years of the 17th century, that number had doubled. Trade and religion went hand in hand—often, Portuguese ships would not enter the harbors of daimyo who opposed Christianity—so the local rulers were forced to put up with the missionaries if they wanted to acquire European goods, such as firearms. A few daimyo even converted to Catholicism, and in 1582 three of them sent an envoy to the pope in Rome.

As the Portuguese presence grew, Japan underwent a process of reunification under a series of powerful warlords. Beginning in 1560, a daimyo named Oda Nobunaga fought to suppress rebellions and conflicts in many parts of Japan. His goal was to bring the country together again under one leader.

Nobunaga was assassinated in 1582 before he could accomplish this goal, but one of his commanders, Toyotomi Hideyoshi, completed the campaign he had begun. In 1590, Hideyoshi took control of the entire country. He reorganized land ownership in the empire, ordered that taxes be paid in rice instead of in silver, and led unsuccessful military expeditions against Korea in 1592 and 1598. He also acted to reduce the missionaries' influence, which the Japanese had begun to regard as a threat. In 1587, he banished all Christian missionaries, and in 1597, he enforced his decree by crucifying 6 European and 20 Japanese Christians.

After Hideyoshi's death, the daimyo fought over the succession at the Battle of Sekigahara. Tokugawa Ieyasu emerged victorious. The daimyo pledged allegiance to him, and he took the title of shogun in 1603. This marked the beginning of the Tokugawa shogunate, which was to rule Japan for 250 years. Ieyasu moved the capital to Edo, on the site of present-day Tokyo, although the emperor and his court remained in Kyoto. Under Tokugawa rule, Japanese society

Under Hideyoshi's rule, the Japanese paid their taxes in rice rather than in silver.

was similar to the feudal societies of Europe in the Middle Ages. The four social classes—nobility, warriors, farmers, and townspeople—obeyed strict rules of behavior and seldom mingled. Farmers were much like medieval serfs, tied to the land they worked and forbidden to travel or possess swords. Change was frowned upon, and tradition governed every aspect of daily life. A vast network of secret police enabled the shoguns to uncover and stamp out any sign of disloyalty or rebellion.

At first, the Tokugawa shogunate was somewhat friendlier to the European missionaries than Hideyoshi had been. But in 1609, the Dutch established a small trading post on the island of Hirado, off the northwest coast of Kyushu, and the Japanese found that they could now trade with the Europeans without accepting their missionary efforts. The shogunate grew increasingly hostile to Christianity, and in 1617, it renewed Hideyoshi's decree. By 1640, it had killed or banished all missionaries and killed thousands of Japanese Christians or forced them to give up their faith.

These strong anti-Christian acts were part of a general policy aimed at keeping Japan isolated from the rest of the world. The Tokugawa wanted to prevent foreign cultures from contaminating the Japanese way of life—and from undermining their power. To this end, they forbade Japanese people to leave the country and foreigners to enter it. They prevented Portuguese ships from landing in Japan, permitting only the Dutch and the Chinese to have limited trading rights. The Dutch were allowed to land only on a tiny island in Nagasaki Harbor, in Kyushu; any trader who left the island could be executed. Less than a century after the first meeting between Japanese and Europeans, the island empire had slammed the door against the outside world and entered what was to be a long era of seclusion.

The seclusion was not entirely unbroken. In 1720, the Tokugawa lifted a ban on foreign books and allowed Japanese scholars to study Dutch scientific and medical texts. Military leaders eagerly acquired European books on weaponry and warfare. A Japanese-Dutch dictionary, completed in 1796, was the first dictionary of the Japanese language. These concessions enabled the Japanese culture to advance even as its virtual isolation continued.

During this period, Japan's cities grew and an urban culture developed. In the early years of the 18th century, Edo (Tokyo) became the largest city in the world, with a population of more than one million. Merchants, artists, and craftsmen took up residence in the towns and cities, close to the wealthy nobility. Arts and crafts were encouraged, and everyone in the noble and warrior classes cultivated an artistic hobby: writing poetry or plays, arranging flowers, or painting landscapes. Many brilliant artworks from the Tokugawa period survive.

During the late 18th and early 19th centuries, foreign nations, including France, Russia, Great Britain, and the United States, sent many ambassadors and gifts to Japan, hoping to be granted trade rights. But the Tokugawa remained firm in their opposition to outsiders.

Then, in 1853, the United States sent a fleet of four ships under Commodore Matthew C. Perry to Japan. The shogun asked the emperor and the most powerful daimyo for help in repelling the American barbarians, but he was forced to recognize the superior strength of the American forces. In 1854, he signed a treaty granting diplomatic and trade rights to the United States. Two years later, Townsend Harris arrived in Edo to take up his post as the first U.S. consul in Japan. The shogun soon granted similar rights to the Netherlands, Russia, France, and Great Britain.

Not all Japanese were pleased with Japan's new international status. Rallying around the young emperor Mutsuhito, a group of young samurai adopted the slogan "Revere the emperor and drive out the barbarians!" They led uprisings against the Tokugawa in many parts of the country, and in 1867, they overthrew the shogunate and ended Japan's feudal era. For the first time in many centuries, political power was in the hands of the emperor and his advisors. Mutsuhito took the name Meiji, meaning "Enlightened Rule," and his return to power is now called the Meiji Restoration.

The samurai who had helped to overthrow the Tokugawa expected the emperor to banish the foreign embassies and restore Japan's traditional, isolated way of life. But they were unpleasantly surprised when, instead, he set out to modernize and Westernize his

Perry's show of naval strength forced Japan to sign a trade treaty with the U.S.

empire. As part of this policy, he passed laws to abolish the samurai class, to take control of the provinces away from the daimyo, and to create an army drafted from among the farmers and townspeople.

The samurai and daimyo resented these acts and felt that their emperor had betrayed them. By 1877, however, imperial forces had defeated the last and greatest samurai revolt, and Japan's new, enlightened era was well under way.

Meiji set up new political structures based on Western models. Between 1885 and 1890, he appointed a prime minister and a cabinet, drafted a constitution, and held elections for a parliament. He lifted the ban on Christianity, allowing missionaries of many different sects to establish churches in Japan.

The country's military strength and ambitions also grew during the late 19th century. In 1894, Japan went to war with China and won some territory on the Asian mainland; however, France, Germany, and Russia forced it to return this territory to China. A few years later, in 1904, Japan attacked Russia and won some of its territory, including the southern half of the Russian Sakhalin Peninsula. It took over Korea in 1910. During World War I (1914 to 1918), it acquired some of Germany's territories in China and the North Pacific.

Many Japanese were proud of these overseas conquests and approved of their country's growing military strength and international aggressiveness. As their power grew, leaders of the armed forces became impatient with the restrictions placed upon them by the civilian government. In 1931, the army took independent action. Without approval from the Japanese government, it sent soldiers into the Chinese province of Manchuria and set up a state called Manchukuo. The League of Nations (a forerunner of the United Nations) criticized this warlike action, and Japan withdrew from the league. In 1932 and 1936, military leaders assassinated many Japanese government figures, including a prime minister. The political parties rapidly lost control of the government, and in 1941, General Tojo Hideki named himself prime minister and supreme military commander. Japan was formally under military rule.

World War II and After

During the late 1930s, the United States and Great Britain helped the Chinese fight the Japanese in China. Japan wanted the United States to withdraw from Asia, and the United States wanted Japan

Japan's attack on Pearl Harbor launched the United States into World War II.

to halt its conquest of its Asian neighbors. While the two nations were negotiating these issues, Japan took action against the United States. On December 7, 1941, Japanese bombers attacked the U.S. fleet at Pearl Harbor, Hawaii. World War II had spread from Europe to the Pacific.

At first, Japan enjoyed great military success. Within six months of the attack on Pearl Harbor, it had captured Malaya, Singapore, the Dutch East Indies, the Philippines, and Burma. But the tide

turned against the Japanese in June 1942, when the United States Navy destroyed many Japanese aircraft carriers in the Battle of Midway. The Japanese had to withdraw from some of their North Pacific islands in 1943. By 1944, U.S. bombers were within range of Tokyo.

Many Japanese leaders realized that their country could no longer hope to win the war. None of them, however, could come up with an acceptable plan to end it. And no one wanted to break the news of the coming defeat to the Japanese public, which had been told only of the Japanese victories. In 1945, the United States carried out massive fire-bombing raids on every major city but Kyoto. General Tojo's government was deposed, and Japanese politicians tried unsuccessfully to find allies among other nations. A mood of desperation and impending disaster took hold of the Japanese people.

On August 6, 1945, a United States airplane dropped an atomic bomb on the Inland Sea port of Hiroshima. On August 8, the Soviet Union entered the war and marched against the Japanese in Manchuria. And on August 9, the United States dropped a second atomic bomb on the harbor at Nagasaki.

With its cities in ruins, its war fleet sunk, and several hundred thousand of its people dead from the effects of the atomic bombs, Japan had no hope of continuing the war. It surrendered on August

General MacArthur led the Allies in a complete restructuring of postwar Japan.

14. United States troops occupied the islands, and control of the country passed into the hands of General Douglas MacArthur, the supreme commander of allied powers.

MacArthur at once set about rebuilding the devastated nation. Stating that he intended to create a democracy for the Japanese people rather than to punish a defeated enemy, he had political prisoners released from jail and ordered the breakup of militaristic organizations. He required Emperor Hirohito to state officially that he was not a god, saw that the aristocrats lost their titles, encouraged workers to form labor unions, and set up programs to make education available to all Japanese. Together with civilian Japanese leaders, MacArthur drew up a new constitution that deprived the emperor of political power—calling him "a symbol of the State"—and placed this power in a two-house legislative parliament, called the Diet, and a prime minister chosen by the Diet members. Women were given the right to vote and to be elected to the Diet.

To modernize the economy, MacArthur broke up the huge estates of the noble families and allowed peasant farmers to buy the land at low prices. New taxes were introduced to provide the government with a source of income and factory managers were instructed in American manufacturing methods. For several decades, the Japanese were forbidden to import goods from other countries, so that Japanese industry could reestablish itself. During the Korean War of 1950 and 1951, many American troops were stationed in Japan, and the country's economy flourished by providing goods and services for them.

The United States occupation of Japan ended in April 1952. American troops withdrew, and the nation was on its own again. Since then, its government has remained stable and its economy has grown faster than that of any other country in the world.

Life in Japan has changed dramatically since World War II. Ancient traditions are still revered, but many Western customs have been adopted.

People and Culture

Japan has a population of 125,612,000, or 861 people per square mile (332 per square kilometer). Because so much of the land area is mountainous and uninhabitable, the population is concentrated in the lowlands. Hokkaido and central Honshu are the least crowded regions, and the areas around Tokyo and along the Honshu coast of the Inland Sea are the most crowded.

Because of their history of isolation, the Japanese have one of the most homogenous national populations in the world—nearly all of the islands' inhabitants belong to the same ethnic group and share the same racial background and cultural characteristics. The Japanese arrived on the islands thousands of years ago; after the sea rose and the land bridges disappeared, they were protected from invasion or the immigration of other peoples. Today, 98.9 percent of the population is Japanese, about .5 percent is of Korean descent, and the remaining .6 percent is made up of Chinese, Westerners, and people of mixed Japanese and Western descent.

Because the population is so homogenous, most Japanese have many physical features in common. The typical Japanese has straight, black hair, dark brown eyes, and light to medium dark skin with a yellowish tan undertone. One feature that the Japanese share

with many other Asian peoples is the epicanthic fold—the full eye-
lids that give the eyes a narrow or "slanted" appearance. The Japanese tend to be fairly small. Men average about 5 feet, 7 inches (1.67
meters) in height, and women are generally somewhat shorter.

The official language of the country is Japanese. Its closest rela-
tive is Korean, but some experts believe that it also contains a few
elements from the languages of southeast Asia (Vietnamese or Indo-
nesian, for example). Spoken Japanese is not an easy language to
learn, and written Japanese is especially difficult because it uses
three alphabets. Chinese characters, called *kanji*, were introduced to
Japan in about 400 A.D. Japanese words were assigned to these sym-
bols, and about 1,850 of them are still used. Then, in about 800, the
Japanese developed an alphabet of their own, called *katakana*. It is
now used primarily to write foreign names. *Hiragana*, the alphabet

*Written Japanese combines three
different alphabets:* hiragana, kanji,
and katakana.

now used to write most Japanese words, was invented at the beginning of the 10th century.

Written Japanese today consists of hiragana with a bit of katakana and a few kanji thrown in, often in the same newspaper article or street sign. It is written and read from right to left, rather than from left to right as is English—although some Japanese publications now use the left-to-right line.

Spoken Japanese varies from one part of the country to another. Many regional dialects (local versions of the language with unique accents or expressions) exist, and speakers of different dialects may not understand one another. Some of the dialects spoken in the more remote areas of Kyushu and the Ryukyu Islands sound very much as medieval Japanese must have sounded in the 15th or 16th century. But education and mass communications have spread standard Japanese to all parts of the islands, so that today, all Japanese also speak the standard version of their language that developed in and around Tokyo in the late 19th century. Dialects are still spoken among family members and in the villages, but Tokyo Japanese is the language of school, business, and the cities.

Trade and travel between the United States and Japan have increased since World War II; as a result, a growing number of Japanese speak English. In addition, the Japanese have borrowed many words from the English language for which there are no Japanese counterparts. Because most Japanese words end in vowels and none of them contain the "L" sound, borrowed words are modified by adding vowels and removing Ls. "Baseball," for example, is *basuboru* in Japan.

The Ainu of Hokkaido

One group of people in Japan differs in origin from the mainstream Japanese population. This group, the Ainu, inhabited all of Hokkaido before great numbers of Japanese moved northward onto that island in the 19th century. The Japanese inrush overwhelmed the Ainu population, and of the 24,000 or so Ainu who live in Hokkaido today, only a handful are pure-blooded. Most Ainu now resemble the Japanese, whose language and culture they have adopted.

Originally, the Ainu were quite different. Unlike the Japanese, Chinese, and Koreans, the Ainu did not belong to the Mongoloid race, from which most Oriental people are descended. They were short and brown-haired, with more body hair than any other human group (the Japanese have very little body hair). The Ainu may have been the remnants of a very ancient Caucasian culture that once lived in northern Asia. Scientists now believe that they crossed the land bridge from the Sakhalin Peninsula into Hokkaido at about the time that the ancestors of the Japanese were entering from Korea. The Ainu did not multiply and spread like the Japanese, and today they have almost died out. The government is making an effort to preserve relics of their culture and language.

The old Ainu were hunters, fishers, and trappers. (Today, the remaining Ainu work on farms or in the new factories that have been built on the northern island.) They wore heavy fur robes and caps to protect them from the cold Hokkaido winters. The men had heavy beards and the women were tattooed around the mouth so that it looked as if they had moustaches. The Ainu worshipped nature spirits, particularly the spirit of the bear. Their most important religious ritual was the yearly sacrifice of a bear; this custom died out around the turn of the century. Some Ainu now keep tame bears and dance with them at the yearly Fire Festival in July.

Religion

Most Japanese practice two different religions. They follow both the ancient, traditional Shinto beliefs of Japan and the Buddhist beliefs introduced from India and China by way of Korea in the 6th century. The blending of these two religions is apparent in the many Buddhist temples that contain Shinto shrines to local gods. Yellow-robed, shaven-headed Buddhist priests chant *sutras* (Buddhist prayers) next to old Shinto statues decorated with gifts of flowers or balls of colored rice.

Shinto remains a powerful religion, although it lost some of its force when the practice of worshipping the emperor as a god ended after World War II. Shinto means "the way of the gods," and it recognizes millions of gods called *kami*, which may be natural objects or historical figures. Each community has at least one Shinto shrine, often quite old, where a great warrior or mountain spirit is honored. All told, Japan has about 80,000 Shinto shrines.

Some of these holy places are quite large and draw pilgrims from all parts of the country. The biggest collection of Shinto shrines is Ise, on the Pacific coast of Honshu, where thousands of Japanese

Most Japanese practice a combination of Shintoism and Buddhism. Traditionally, people are married in Shinto ceremonies and buried with Buddhist funeral rites.

each year pay their respects to the sun goddess—the mythical founder of the imperial line. By ancient custom, the Ise shrines are torn down and rebuilt every 20 years. A small but very holy Shinto shrine is located on the Inland Sea island of Kashiwa Jima. Once each year, thousands of Japanese converge on the island to worship at its humble shrine. The rest of the time, the island is uninhabited except for one old Shinto priest who periodically dresses in purple and green robes to bless the fishing boats of neighboring islands.

Although many Japanese are married in Shinto ceremonies, most are buried with Buddhist funeral rituals, which feature the chanting of prayers and the hanging of black-and-white striped cloths. Many Japanese feel that Shinto is concerned with daily life and that Buddhism is a preparation for the hereafter. The two religions coexist comfortably, with no conflict between their practices.

Christianity was banned in Japan by the Tokugawa shogunate in the mid-17th century, and the ban was not lifted until the Meiji Restoration in 1873. In the 200 years before the restoration, however, Roman Catholicism survived on remote islands, in western Kyushu, and in a few "hiding Christian" villages. After the restoration, Western missionaries established many Protestant, Russian Orthodox, and Catholic churches. Today, about 1 percent of the Japanese are Christians. Among the Christians, 60 percent are Protestant and 40 percent are Catholic.

The final and smallest element of Japan's religious life is the so-called "new religions" that have sprung up during the last 100 years. Most of them are mixtures of beliefs and practices from the Shinto, Buddhist, and Christian faiths. One of the largest is the Soka Gakkai (Value Creation Society). Based on a Buddhist sect, the Soka Gakkai has become a powerful political organization. Other new religions are the Tenri-kyo (Religion of Divine Wisdom) and the Rissho Kosei-kai (Society for Establishing Righteousness and Friendly Relations).

(continued on page 65)

Scenes of
JAPAN

➤ *Rice, for centuries Japan's staple crop, is now harvested with modern machinery.*

∨ *Mt. Fuji, Japan's highest point, rises majestically from the island of Honshu.*

▲ *Spanning the Seto Inland Sea, the Onaruto Bridge is part of Japan's modern road system.*

◄ *Land for housing is at a premium on the crowded islands.*

Japan is the world's largest producer of robots. This robot welds auto parts.

◄ *Many Japanese artworks, like this painted wood-block print, reflect ancient customs or ways of life. Shown here is a procession of feudal lords and their attendants.*

▼ *Nearly all Japanese children attend kindergarten, even though they are not required to.*

⋏ *Sportsmen find Japan's mountains to be ideal for skiing, climbing, and hiking.*

➤ *The art of flower arranging, called* ikebana, *is part of Japan's artistic tradition.*

◄ *Tokyo, the capital, is one of the world's largest cities.*

∀ *Sumo, a popular form of wrestling, dates from the 1st century B.C. The object is for one wrestler to throw the other to the ground or push him out of the ring.*

➤ *Kabuki theater, in which all roles are played by men, has been produced since 1603.*

⌄ *Youngsters play team sports, such as soccer, during physical education classes.*

(continued from page 56)

Family Life

Many traditional customs of Japanese family life have been largely replaced by more modern, Western ways. The degree of Westernization varies, but almost no aspect of daily life remains unchanged.

Marriage is one example of a practice in transition from Eastern to Western ways. Traditionally, Japanese men and women did not choose their marriage partners on the basis of romantic love. Instead, marriages were arranged by matchmakers, who paired couples on the basis of their families' social and economic status. Neighborhood groups, labor organizations to which the groom or the parents belonged, and the community in general were expected to give their opinions about the suitability of the marriage.

This practice is still widespread among the Japanese, in the cities as well as in the more traditional countryside, and each community has several matchmakers who specialize in finding mates for unmarried young men and women. But it is becoming more common for men and women to make the decision to marry without the help of the matchmakers, often for emotional reasons as much as practical ones. Even in romantic marriages, however, the approval of both families is considered essential. Very few Japanese would dream of defying their families with an "unsuitable" marriage to someone of a different economic or social background.

Dating was almost unknown in Japan until recent years, when more and more single women entered the work force and had the opportunity to meet men outside their families. Today, some younger Japanese go on dates like those of Western teenagers, although group outings are more common.

The role of girls and women has become more liberated in the past few decades. Before World War II, peasant women worked in the family fields but women were not expected to have jobs of their own. Now, more women, especially in the larger cities, have careers. Under Japanese law, women have the same rights to education and

Modern Japanese families tend to be small, usually with one or two children.

employment as men, and these rights are starting to be carried out in practice.

Once married, Japanese couples used to live with—or at least close to—the husband's family. Today, most couples have homes or apartments of their own. Because family ties are still quite important, it is not unusual for grandparents and other family members to make frequent visits. Families are smaller than they used to be, usually with one or two children instead of four or five. (The Japanese are trying to keep their population from growing much larger.)

Clothing is one area in which tradition has been almost completely abandoned in favor of Western styles. Men used to wear long, flowing robes, made of silk if they were wealthy and of plain, quilted cotton if they were poor. Women dressed in *kimonos*, floor-length, long-sleeved gowns held in place by wide sashes, called *obis*, tied around the waist. Some kimonos of dyed and embroidered silk were lovely works of art.

Today, however, few Japanese wear these traditional garments in public, except on ceremonial or religious occasions or holidays. Businessmen wear Western-style suits, usually black, with white shirts and black ties. Workmen wear pants and shirts. Women wear dresses or skirts and blouses. Schoolchildren wear uniforms of white shirts or blouses and dark pants or skirts. At home, though, many

Japanese relax in kimonos or loose robes called *hapi* coats. Bluejeans and T-shirts are favorite leisure clothes for teenagers.

Some Western-style foods—such as spaghetti and McDonald's hamburgers—are popular in Japan's large cities, but most Japanese food is very traditional. The Japanese have always favored a diet rich in seafood and have developed many ways to prepare and eat the abundant marine life from the waters around the islands.

Japanese seafood includes tuna, mackerel, and swordfish, as well as squid, octopus, eel, shrimp, oysters, and lobster. *Sashimi* (tiny pieces of raw seafood served with spicy horseradish paste or soy sauce) and *sushi* (bite-sized sashimi wrapped around cold rice with strips of seaweed) are two Japanese specialties that are now available

Few women wear kimonos. Western clothing has replaced traditional styles.

in many American and European cities. One seafood specialty found only in Japan is *fugu*. Regarded as a great delicacy, fugu is made from a poisonous variety of blowfish and must be prepared with extraordinary care to ensure that the servings contain no poison. Under Japanese law, fugu can be prepared only by specially licensed chefs. Nevertheless, eating fugu is a gamble with death. It is so delicious that it remains one of the country's favorite foods, even though several dozen Japanese die from fugu poisoning each year.

Soups of all kinds, from the clear broth called *miso* to the hearty winter stew called *nabemono*, are popular. Beef is served in some Japanese restaurants, but portions tend to be small as beef is very expensive (due to the scarcity of grazing land). *Yakitori* (grilled chicken) and *ramen* (noodles) are typical inexpensive meals.

The Japanese prize the appearance of their food almost as much as its taste. Even casual or low-priced meals are artfully arranged— the pieces of food form a design decorated with bits of carved raw vegetables or tiny dishes of sauce. Elaborate meals in the finest restaurants are considered works of art and are eaten slowly and in silence—with chopsticks, as are all Japanese meals. The Japanese people have adopted a blend of the traditional East and the modern West in many aspects of daily life, but they have not replaced the chopsticks with the knife and fork.

Arts and Culture

Japan has a long artistic tradition. The earliest relics of Japanese civilization are decorated pottery pieces and fragments. In the early 17th century, tea-drinking had become so popular that powerful daimyo kidnapped hundreds of skilled potters from Korea to set up kilns and pottery workshops to produce teacups on the feudal estates. Today, Japanese artists still take pride in creating beautiful pottery and ceramics. Kyoto is especially famous for its elegant blue-and-white porcelains and colorful, enameled clay jars and bowls.

Craftsmen carve elaborate statues from hardwoods. Wood carving is an ancient art.

Weaving is another ancient art that is still practiced, particularly in the rural areas. Textile arts and crafts range from simple, home-spun mufflers to elaborate, formal kimonos and obis, decorated with silver and gold thread, silk brocade, and hundreds of carefully shaded dyes. The Japanese have always practiced woodworking as well, and today, fine furniture and artwork made from Japanese hardwoods are prized all over the world. Japanese cabinets and other wood pieces are noted for their coatings of hard, shiny lacquer, usually black and decorated with designs in gold or silver—this type of finish, in fact, is sometimes called japanning. The finest lacquering is done by hand, according to secret processes handed down from father to son.

Other uniquely Japanese handicrafts include dolls dressed in traditional ceremonial costumes (meant for display rather than play), combs carved from beechwood, lunchboxes and other containers woven from strips of pine and cherry bark, and painted paper lanterns and umbrellas. *Origami*, a Japanese art form familiar to many Westerners, is the art of making small shapes of animals or other figures by folding bits of colored paper.

Today, many of these traditional arts and crafts are dying out as factory production replaces individual workmanship and young people lose interest in the skills of older generations. In 1955, the government began a program to preserve its cultural heritage by identifying dedicated artists and craftspeople as National Living Treasures. These individuals receive funds from the Agency for Cultural Affairs to help them continue to practice their crafts. The government also buys their best works for national museums and sponsors apprenticeship programs for youngsters who want to study under them.

Not all of the National Living Treasures produce handicrafts. Some are involved in Japan's many unique performing arts, such as the Kabuki theater. Created by the master playwright Chikamatsu Monzaemon in the 17th century, Kabuki features as many as 50 actors (with women's roles played by men) performing stories based on Japanese legends of love and war. Spectacular sound and music effects, and sometimes dancing and singing, accompany the performances.

This elaborate, inlaid box is another example of handcrafted Japanese woodwork.

In Bunraku, large puppets act out stories while a narrator explains the performance. Just as in Kabuki, only men may participate in Bunraku.

Similar to Kabuki are the Bunraku theater and the Noh theater. In Bunraku theater, stories are acted by puppets to the accompaniment of a narrator and a musician; the Noh theater specializes in producing slow-moving plays based on old-fashioned aristocratic life and features actors who paint their faces white or wear complicated masks that have different meanings. Japan is developing more modern, Western-style plays, but it is also trying to keep its traditional theaters alive. The government-funded National Theater produces both modern and traditional plays.

Dance and music were once studied by all Japanese and are still an important part of the culture. The traditional Japanese instruments are the guitar-like *shamisen* and the *koto*, similar to a horizontal harp. Today, Japan has several Western-style symphony orchestras, and Western music, especially jazz, is popular. Rock stars from the United States and Great Britain are immensely admired by

Japan's young people, who flock to their performances from all over the country.

Many of Japan's museums possess centuries-old paintings or wood-block prints (pictures made by carving a design into a piece of wood, inking the raised portions of the wood, and then pressing the block to a sheet of parchment). The typical Japanese style of drawing

The government is trying to preserve Japan's ancient artworks.

and painting is delicate, with fine lines similar to the lines in Japanese writing. Landscapes, close-ups of flowers, and historic scenes are among the traditional subjects, but more modern artists are experimenting with abstract oil painting and other Western forms.

Japan has many museums and workshops that exhibit arts and crafts, and its department stores also provide an important opportunity for artists to show their work. Most stores sponsor frequent, free art exhibitions. Many of them also use artworks as decoration. It is not unusual for people to come to the stores just to look at a display of pictures or pottery.

In the field of literary arts, Japan is noted as the home of the world's first novel, *The Tale of Genji*. Written by a court lady, Murasaki Shikibu, in about 1000 A.D., it tells of the love affairs of Prince Genji and is famous for its detailed and witty portrayal of court life in medieval Japan. Literature blossomed after the Japanese alphabet was developed, and the 8th century brought forth Japan's first written history, called the *Kojiki* (which today is prized for its accounts of early emperors and dealings with Korea and China), and its first collection of poetry, the *Manyoshu* (Collection of ten thousand leaves).

Later, Japanese poets developed several kinds of poems found only in Japan. The best known is the *haiku*, a short poem of 17 syllables in three lines. A good haiku is supposed to suggest both a scene and a mood, often one of thoughtfulness, sadness, or nostalgia. This haiku, written about the ancient Tomoe Inn in the small samurai town of Hagi, is typical:

> A courtyard window
> This tree stands, remembering
> The old Tomoe.

Other uniquely Japanese art forms include *ikebana* (the art of flower arranging), the *chanoyu* (an elaborate tea ceremony with

Baseball is as popular in Japan as it is in the United States—if not more so.

ritual gestures), and the carving of *netsuke* (small jade or ivory figures used to weight the ends of sashes and obis). These arts developed during the flourishing of court life at Nara and Heian between the 8th and 12th centuries, and all are practiced to some extent today.

Leisure Time

The Japanese are fond of sports and physical activity. Many people, old and young alike, practice one or more of the martial arts invented in Japan: *karate* (fighting by striking and kicking), *judo* (similar to wrestling), *kendo* (stick fighting), and *aikido* (defeating an opponent by avoiding his attacks).

Western sports, especially baseball, have become very popular in Japan. The Japanese regard their ball players as popular heroes, much like rock stars in the United States. Soccer, golf, and tennis have also begun to catch on among the younger Japanese.

Perhaps the most popular leisure-time activity, however, is gardening. The Japanese love gardens, and even those who live in apartments usually have windowboxes, alcoves for potted plants, or roof gardens. Almost every Japanese house has at least one 6-foot-by-6-foot (2-meter-by-2-meter) garden, often containing nothing more than a single tree or bamboo plant, one or two large rocks, and sand or gravel raked into pleasing patterns. Another form of gardening is the raising of bonsai, miniature trees that grow only inches (centimeters) high and are painstakingly trained into artistic shapes.

Tokyo, one of the world's largest cities, began as a feudal fortress, or joka-machi *(castle-town). The Japanese consider the city to be "the heart of Japan."*

Cities, Villages, and Countryside

Slightly more than three-fourths of Japan's people live in cities; the rest live in rural villages or the countryside. The cities have grown greatly in the years since World War II, as young people have left their rural villages in search of better jobs and more modern lifestyles. Some small villages have been completely abandoned and are falling into decay. This is especially common in the central part of Honshu. Demographers (people who study the development and movement of populations) predict that the drift of people from Japan's countryside into its cities will continue.

Many of Japan's towns and cities, including Tokyo, started out as *joka-machi* (castle-towns), fortresses built by the feudal warlords to control travel and trade routes, mountain passes, and harbors. As the shoguns and daimyo gathered craftsmen and merchants around them, urban centers developed. Ports (such as Nagasaki) and religious temples or shrines (such as Nara) also grew into cities over the centuries. Today, Japan's cities face the problems of urban centers all over the world: pollution, crowding, traffic jams, and crime. But they are also exciting centers of business, banking, and the arts, crammed with historical and religious sites, as well as gardens and parks.

Tokyo, Japan's capital, is one of the world's largest cities, with a population of 7,962,000. Its two international airports are among the world's busiest, and its streets and subway trains are always crowded. Because earthquakes devastated the city in 1923 and wartime raids did so in 1945, many of its buildings are new. The emperor's palace, which once stood on the site of Tokugawa Ieyasu's old castle, was destroyed in the war. A new palace was completed in 1968.

Southeast of the Imperial Palace is the heart of Tokyo's business, shopping, and entertainment district. Sometimes called Shimbashi, this part of the city contains the famous Ginza Strip, a neon-

Tokyo was rebuilt after air raids destroyed much of it during World War II.

lit thoroughfare of restaurants, bars, and stores that is thronged with Japanese and tourists day and night. The area contains a number of enormous, Western-style department stores, called *deparatos* by the Japanese.

Tokyo is both the seat of government and the center of business. The parliament and dozens of other government buildings line the streets south and west of the palace grounds. To the east is the financial and business district, with the soaring steel-and-glass skyscrapers of the country's large corporations: Sony, Mitsubishi, Kawasaki, and others. But not all of Tokyo is bustling and modern. The city has many temples, shrines, and quiet parks, as well as a few old neighborhoods where narrow, twisting streets and old, wooden houses have survived both earthquakes and war.

Many more such neighborhoods can be found in Kyoto, the only major Japanese city that was not bombed during World War II. As Heian, Kyoto was the center of Japanese culture, religion, and tradition for 1,000 years. The Japanese call the city "Nihon no furusato" (the heart of Japan).

Kyoto has more than 2,000 temples, shrines, palaces, and gardens. Many of them are clustered along the Old Canal, a waterway that runs through the city and is shaded with graceful cherry trees. The Ginkakuji, or Silver Pavilion, built in 1479 by Ashikaga Yoshimasa and later made into a Zen Buddhist temple, is one of the country's most famous shrines. Its main courtyard contains a garden made of piles of sand. Designed to be viewed by moonlight, the sand garden is said to represent the lakes of China. Many thousands of Japanese visit Kyoto each year to explore the Ginkakuji and other relics of their past.

Osaka, south of Kyoto on the Inland Sea, arose as a cultural and political center between the 5th and 8th centuries, when Korean and Chinese influences entered Honshu by way of Kyushu and the Inland Sea. Osaka's cemetery of Nintoku, one of the early emperors, is believed to be the largest cemetery in the world. Another historical site in Osaka contains some of the towers and walls of the immense castle built by Toyotomi Hideyoshi at the peak of his power. More than 7 miles (11 kilometers) around, the castle required three years of labor from 63,000 men.

Today, Osaka is the business hub of the industrial strip that runs along the Inland Sea's western coast. It is the center of Japan's textile and chemical industries and the outgoing port for about 40 percent of the country's exports. And Osaka's 35,000 restaurants have earned it the nickname "the city of restaurants." Some high-rise buildings are devoted entirely to restaurants, with a different type of food served on each floor.

Other Japanese cities include Yokohama, on the eastern coast, once a quiet fishing village and now the second largest city in the country; Sapporo, the capital city of Hokkaido, built only a century ago and host of the 1972 Winter Olympic Games; Nagoya, a modern city that has grown up in the middle of the Tokaido (the "eastern sea road," the name given to the densely populated industrial and economic belt that stretches from Tokyo to Hiroshima); and Kobe, Japan's busiest port and home to many of the country's foreign residents.

Japan still has many small towns and rural villages, although their populations are slowly shrinking. Some of the towns look much as they did during Japan's feudal era. Hagi, on the west coast of Honshu, is a quiet town of steep streets, white houses with tile roofs, simple gardens, and pine trees. It contains many old samurai houses and schools, including those of the samurai teacher Yoshida Shoin, who started the Meiji Restoration.

Other small towns are scattered through the islands, particularly in their western and central regions. Many artists and craftsmen live in these old-fashioned, traditional towns, which often have ancient shrines and cozy inns to attract travelers.

Most villages have between 30 and 50 families, who share the labor and benefits of working the village fields or rice paddies. These rural communities are called *mura*. Villages in Hokkaido are dependent on commercial agriculture—residents work on large farms operated as businesses rather than on their own small plots of land. In southwestern Japan, many villages are based on fishing. The fishermen sell their catches to dealers, who in turn transport the fish

Only a few remote villages remain unchanged since the days of the shoguns. Most towns now feature modern architecture and industries.

to the large cities or to canneries. In the mountainous central Honshu region, a handful of villages still survive by logging, hunting, and making and selling charcoal.

Although they remain traditional in many ways, Japan's villages are not isolated from city life. Those close to large, urban centers have many commuters, who work in the cities but return in the evenings. More remote villages send seasonal laborers to the cities during the winter, when there are no crops to tend. And almost all villagers have telephones, radios, and television sets.

Traditional Japanese houses consisted of wooden frames and roofs and sliding wall panels of heavy paper. They contained very little furniture—only cotton quilts, called *futons*, for sleeping, and wooden chests for storing clothing and other items. The floors were covered with *tatami*, mats of woven reeds or straw. Some of these houses still stand in small towns and even in the largest cities, but today most Japanese houses and furniture are more modern and Western in style. People in the cities live in apartments and people in small towns and villages often have small houses of brick, wood, or painted concrete. But whether traditional or modern, whether in apartments or inns, Japanese rooms still have tatami flooring, and the Japanese still remove their shoes at the door and step into *geta* (slippers) before entering.

Despite its dense population, Japan has a great deal of uninhabited and undeveloped countryside. Mountainous and rugged, much of it will probably never be settled. The Japanese, proud of their country's natural beauty and eager to preserve it, have created 28 national parks up and down the islands, from Hokkaido to the Ryukyu Islands. These parks attract thousands of Japanese and foreign tourists every year. Among the most interesting national parks are Daisetsuzan, in Hokkaido, the largest park, filled with volcanoes, pine-covered mountains, deep gorges, torrential streams, and hot springs; Hakone, which includes Mount Fuji; the Minami Alps, featuring many hiking trails and climbing routes; and Seto Naikai, along the Inland Sea.

Japan's government and local fishing associations work together to protect the country's marine life in about 160 undersea parks. These marine parks range from coral reefs south of Okinawa to Izu Park, an undersea sanctuary near Tokyo that is home to the giant spider crab, the world's largest crustacean. Sometimes called *shinin gani* (dead man's crab) because it is believed to eat the corpses of drowned sailors, the giant crab measures 11 feet (3.3 meters) across from claw to claw.

In addition to protecting the land and wildlife, Japan's parks offer recreational opportunities. Spring weekends are perfect for admiring flowers and cherry blossoms and summer weekends are ideal for picnicking. In the autumn, visitors hike the parks' trails to see the brilliantly colored leaves. Winter weekends find hundreds of Japanese lined up at the ski runs in the Japan Alps.

Japan's legislative body, the bicameral Diet, meets in this building in Tokyo. The nation's governmental structure was laid out in the constitution of 1947.

Government Services

Japan's current constitution came into effect in 1947. Intended to prevent the kind of militaristic leadership that had made Japan so warlike during the first half of the 20th century, the 1947 constitution guarantees the rights of the people in a statement similar to the United States Bill of Rights. In addition, it states that the emperor is not a god but merely a symbol of the Japanese state, that the prime minister and all of the cabinet ministers must be civilians, and that Japan will never maintain an army, a navy, or an air force.

Since 1947, Japan has created a military defense force of about 240,000 people. The constitution defines the military's role as strictly one of self-defense. In recent years, however, Japan has gradually allowed its military to play a somewhat larger role. For example, Japanese troops can now participate in United Nations peacekeeping missions.

The 1947 constitution established a three-branch system of government similar to that of the United States. The executive branch is headed by the prime minister. The prime minister is elected by the Diet, from among its members, and then officially appointed by the emperor. He is assisted in his duties by 20 ministers of areas such as finance, trade and industry, and economic planning. These ministers, along with the prime minister, form the cabinet.

The Diet's responsibilities changed dramatically after World War II.

The Diet, Japan's legislative body, consists of two houses. Members of the House of Representatives are elected to four-year terms, and members of the House of Councillors to six-year terms. The House of Representatives, the larger and more powerful body, controls the national budget and approves treaties with foreign powers.

The judicial branch consists of a supreme court, 8 high courts, 47 district courts, and many smaller courts. The cabinet appoints justices of the courts to ten-year terms. Japan does not use the jury system; cases are decided by the justices.

For administrative purposes, Japan is divided into 47 districts called prefectures; 43 of them are similar in size and shape, 1 of them consists of the entire island of Hokkaido, 2 are the urban areas of Osaka and Kyoto, and 1 is the metropolitan district of greater Tokyo. The prefectures are administered by elected governors and assemblies and are further subdivided into cities, towns, and villages, each of which elects its own mayor and assembly.

The constitution gives Japan's citizens the right to form any number of political parties. At present, the country has more than 10,000 parties, although many are quite small and have no real power. The largest and most powerful is the Liberal Democratic party (LDP), which has led the government for the most part since 1955. Moderately conservative, it favors slow, gradual development rather than extreme changes in policy. The Liberal Democratic party has been largely responsible for Japan's political and economic stability in the decades since World War II.

Other important parties include the Social Democratic party (SDP) and Shinshinto, or the New Frontier party (NFP). Shinshinto was formed in 1994 by the merger of several different parties. Typically each of these groups wins some seats in the Diet at each election, along with various minor parties. All Japanese citizens over age 20 are eligible to vote in national, prefectural, and local elections. In recent years, turnout for national elections has commonly reached 60 percent or more of the eligible voters.

Education

Japan is one of the few countries in the world with a literacy rate of 100 percent. All Japanese over age 15 can read and write. The Japanese school system is modern and well funded, and the people believe strongly in the value of education. The country devotes more than 8 percent of its budget to education every year and has an ample supply of schools and teachers. Most Japanese children enjoy school and eagerly compete for scholarships and academic prizes.

A child's education begins at age three, with three years of kindergarten. Although attending kindergarten is not required by law, nearly all children attend. After kindergarten come six years of elementary school, three years of middle school (similar to junior high school in the United States), and three years of high school. Students are required by law to attend school for the first nine years. High school is not compulsory, but everyone attends anyway.

Physical education classes are part of the curriculum in Japan's excellent, modern schools.

In classes averaging no more than 20 people, Japanese school-children study many of the same subjects as students in the United States or Europe do, including history, biology, and social science. They tend to spend more time on mathematics and science than do children in Western schools. Nearly all of them study English for five years in middle school and high school because the college entrance exams include a written test in English. As a result, most teenagers in Japan speak some English and are eager to practice it with tourists. The students also study some traditional Japanese subjects, such as calligraphy, the art of drawing Japanese and Chinese characters with a brush and ink. Most children have at least three hours of homework every night, and more on weekends.

After high school, students must pass extremely difficult and competitive entrance examinations in order to go to college. Many special schools, called *juku*, have been set up to help young people prepare for these tests. More than 590 junior colleges offer two- or three-year study programs, and more than 570 colleges and universities offer four-year programs. Some five-year technical colleges combine high school and junior college. During the 1970s, the government built the Tsukuba Science City, a complex of two universities and some research laboratories, about 40 miles (64 kilometers) north of Tokyo.

Health

Japan's population is a healthy one. Men live about 77 years on average, women nearly 83. Diseases such as tuberculosis and small-pox, which ravaged the population after the Europeans introduced them, have been wiped out. Today, the major causes of death are cancer, heart and lung diseases, and pneumonia. The country has one of the largest and most efficient health-care systems in the world, with a doctor for every 546 people and a hospital bed for every 75 people.

Medical science and treatment in Japan are generally similar to those of Western hospitals. Equipment is modern and medicines are widely available. But some doctors and hospitals, in metropolitan areas as well as small towns, combine Western science with classical Chinese medical treatments such as acupuncture (sticking tiny needles just under the surface of the skin at certain points of the body to relieve pain) and herbal potions (teas or ointments made of herbs according to ancient recipes). Many doctors and patients claim that these remedies bring as much relief as more modern methods.

Doctors and scientists all over the world began studying the Japanese diet in the 1960s, when they noticed that the Japanese had unusually low rates of certain kinds of cancer and heart disease. They determined that the traditional diet—based on rice and fish with little red meat, fat, or sugar—helped to prevent these diseases from developing. As their standard of living has increased, however, the Japanese have begun to eat more fatty foods and sugars. As a result, there are now more incidences of colon cancer and hardened arteries, although the rates of these diseases are still lower than in the industrialized nations of the West.

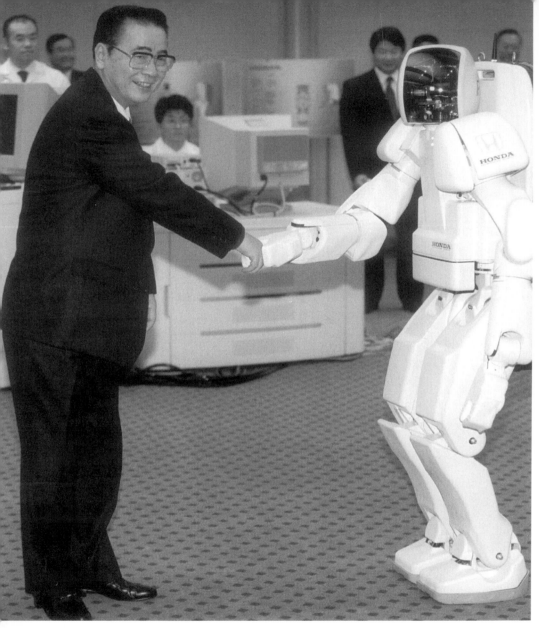

P3, a robot developed by the Japanese company Honda, shakes hands with Chinese Premier Li Peng. Japan is a world leader in technology.

Resources and Economy

Japan has few natural resources. Only about 15 percent of the land is suitable for farming, and much of this is covered with settlements or industrial development. The many rivers of the mountain regions could provide much hydroelectric energy, but building dams and power plants in such remote and rugged terrain is difficult and expensive. Coal is mined in Hokkaido and Kyushu, but it is of poor quality and insufficient to meet the country's needs. Petroleum, iron ore, copper, and other materials needed for an industrial economy must be imported.

Despite its shortage of natural resources, Japan has one of the world's most productive economies. It fills 42 percent of its food needs with crops grown on fewer than 13 million cultivated acres (5.1 million hectares). Its manufacturing and trade production is second only to that of the United States.

Japan's chief products are ships, steel (made from imported raw materials), automobiles, electronic equipment (computers and telecommunications devices), and consumer electronic goods (stereos, cameras, televisions, and other appliances). The country is also the world's largest producer of robots and automated machinery—in fact, several factories are entirely operated by robots building other robots. The textile and lumber industries have grown more slowly than the high-technology fields, but they remain important. Japan also has one of the world's largest fishing industries, composed mainly of families or small businesses, along with a few large commercial fleets. Much of the annual catch is used to supply the country's own food needs, although some seafood is sold abroad.

Part of Japan's success in rebuilding its shattered economy after World War II is due to the country's unique system of close cooperation between business and government. A board called the Economic Planning Agency, made up of members of government agencies and leading industries and corporations, sets economic goals and makes plans to reach them. Government and business regard themselves as partners in Japan's development.

Another important aspect of economic life in Japan is the relationship between the big manufacturing corporations and the people who work for them. When a man—or woman, although fewer women than men hold corporate or factory jobs—goes to work for a company, he becomes part of a "family." Often the company will sell him a house or rent him an apartment at a low rate. Some companies even have whole suburbs or small cities for their employees to live in. The company may provide scholarships for a worker's children, vacations for his whole family, and yearly parties or festivals. People in Japan expect to work for the same company for their entire career—jumping from job to job is unusual. The companies want to make their employees happy and productive, and employees expect to be taken care of for life by their company. This system has produced the world's highest rate of industrial output per worker.

In the 1980s, businesses in the United States and Europe suffered from competition with Japanese industry. The Japanese were able to produce high-quality goods at a lower cost than other countries could manage. Many business executives visited Japan to study

Journalists examine a new Toyota. Automobiles are one of Japan's major products.

its manufacturing methods and, particularly, its system of employee relations. Some aspects of this system were actually invented in the United States but put into practice in Japan, including granting factory workers representation in corporate planning meetings, letting employees form committees to solve problems and assign tasks rather than receiving orders from management, and rewarding good suggestions with money or promotions. Some of these methods have recently been adopted by companies in other countries.

One aspect of Japan's economic system is causing problems with other nations, especially the United States. This is its policy of protectionism—imposing heavy taxes on imported goods to encourage the growth of Japanese industry. After World War II, protectionism enabled Japan to develop its own industries instead of running up

Shigeru Miyamoto, creator of Super Mario video games, operates Super Mario 64, one of Japan's popular export products.

debts by buying products from other nations. The policy worked—perhaps too well. Now Japan sells much more to other countries than it buys from them, which hurts the other countries' economies.

Although Japan is the United States's biggest customer for agricultural products and equipment, the United States has a trade deficit of over $59 billion with Japan. This means that the United States spends far more for goods from Japan than Japan spends on U.S. products. American manufacturers suffer because Japan's high import taxes (called tariffs) prevent them from selling their products for a reasonable price in Japan, while Japanese products are imported cheaply into the United States, which has low import taxes. Adjusting the tariffs so that trade can be more balanced is the single biggest item of discussion between the two countries today. Other nations, particularly in industrial Western Europe, are also concerned about reducing their trade deficits with Japan.

Balanced trade has been achieved in one important industry: tourism. Each year, thousands of Japanese visit Europe, the United States, Asia, and the Pacific countries, usually in organized tour groups. And thousands of foreign visitors descend upon the shrines, palaces, parks, and inns of Japan. By the mid-1990s, visitors from the United States alone were spending $3.5 billion a year in Japan. The number of visitors to Japan is expected to keep growing.

The Japanese unit of currency is the *yen*, divided into 100 *sen*. In 1996, the United States dollar was equal to about 112 yen. The yearly income of the average Japanese family is about 6,850,000 yen, equal to about U.S. $61,000. Most of these earnings are spent on food and taxes (income and sales taxes are high in Japan), or put into savings (the average Japanese family saves almost 13 percent of its earnings). Housing and furniture costs are relatively low—a typical family spends as much on books and recreation in a year as on rent or mortgage payments. Education and medical care are paid for almost entirely by government programs, so these expenses are not great.

Most Japanese live fairly comfortably. Almost every household has a telephone, a washing machine, a refrigerator, and a color television. Although the incomes of rural farmers, coastal fishermen, small shopkeepers, and some factory workers are at the low end of the scale, there is little or no true poverty. Slums, begging, and homeless people are all but nonexistent. All Japanese feel a strong obligation to take care of even their distant relatives, and the government provides low-cost housing and jobs for the needy.

The government-owned national rail system carries millions of passengers each year. Although overcrowding is a problem, the system is quite efficient.

Transportation and Communications

Until the late 19th century, most Japanese traveled on foot. The only vehicles were small wagons or *kago* (stretcher-like carriers, with silk curtains, in which wealthy or aristocratic passengers were carried by men or animals). In 1872, under Emperor Meiji, the first railway was built between Tokyo and Yokohama. Today, Japan boasts one of the most modern and thorough transportation systems in the world.

The railways remain the most developed form of transportation in Japan. The government owns the national rail system, and private companies operate additional commuter trains in the larger cities. Despite constant expansion, the commuter trains are almost always crowded. During rush hour, they carry two or three times the number of passengers they were meant to hold. The Japanese are good-natured about this crowding, however, and cheerfully allow themselves to be packed tightly into the cars by railroad employees hired for that purpose.

Japan has 16,720 miles (26,908 kilometers) of railways. The best-known trains are the famous Shinkansen, or "bullet trains." These high-speed vehicles cover the 325 miles (520 km) between Tokyo and Osaka in three hours. The Shinkansen also run from Tokyo to Honshu and Kyushu.

In recent years, the number of cars and trucks in Japan has increased greatly. Today, the country has about 43 million automobiles—80 percent of all families own cars. More than 20 million trucks carry cargo along the nation's highways, and motorcycles, scooters, and motorized bicycles are everywhere. Most city streets are a pandemonium of screeching brakes, revving motors, and blaring horns, with students on motorcycles or bicycles, carrying their books on their backs, weaving among the slow-moving cars. The country has 706,091 miles (1,136,346 kilometers) of roads; about three-quarters of them are paved. The road system is now growing faster than the rail system, and aside from some of the national parkland, virtually all parts of the islands are accessible by road.

Travel from island to island—once possible only by sea—has become simpler in the 20th century. In 1941, the world's first undersea railway tunnel was built between Honshu and Kyushu. Today, a double-decked undersea roadway and a suspension bridge also connect the two islands. In 1983, the world's longest undersea railway tunnel was completed between Honshu and Hokkaido. Three large bridges link Honshu and Shikoku.

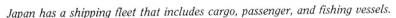

Japan has a shipping fleet that includes cargo, passenger, and fishing vessels.

Air travel among the islands is also increasing. Southwestern Japan has more small, local airports than other parts of the country because its many islands are best served by air travel and cargo transport. Japan Air Lines is the national airline, owned by the government. Most international travel to and from Japan is by air. Tokyo, with two international airports in its suburbs, is the largest air traffic center, followed by Osaka, Nagoya, Sapporo, and Fukuoka. All major world airlines provide service to Japan.

Japan is one of the world's leading seafaring nations, with a fleet of 7,165 merchant (cargo) ships and major ports at Kobe, Yokohama, and Nagoya. Kitakyushu serves sea traffic to western Kyushu, and Hiroshima is an important port for the southern part of the Inland Sea.

Japan's communications systems are as well developed as its transportation. Its three largest newspapers, *Yomiuri Shimbun*, *Asahi Shimbun*, and *Mainichi Shimbun*, each has a daily circulation of 4 million to 10 million. The total combined circulation of all the country's 121 daily newspapers is 72.5 million, or more than half of the country's population. Almost everyone old enough to read sees at least part of a newspaper every day. In addition, Japan has one of the world's largest publishing industries, producing more than 5,100 magazines and more than 63,000 new books each year (more than are published in the United States).

Japan has more radio and television stations and sets than any other Asian country. The government sponsors the biggest radio station (founded in 1925) and the biggest television station (founded in 1952). These stations, both called NHK, do not broadcast commercials. Many privately owned stations, paid for with commercials, offer alternative programs to local or national audiences.

Japanese society is a fascinating blend of the old and the new. Ancient traditions such as Noh theater survive, even as the nation forges into the future.

Around the Islands

Japan today is a colorful, sometimes bewildering blend of old and new, East and West. It is a land where businessmen in Western suits greet each other with formal bows instead of handshakes, where ancient palaces rub shoulders with towering skyscrapers, where people travel on high-speed trains to make walking pilgrimages to Shinto shrines. Everywhere in the islands, reminders of Japan's past mingle with the activities of the present.

On the northern island of Hokkaido, people still celebrate winter as the old Ainu did—with an elaborate annual Snow Festival featuring hundreds of sculptures in snow and ice. Today, however, television cameras and movie crews light up the night to photograph the glittering, block-long ice palaces and snow bears.

At the southern tip of Hokkaido, Japan's northernmost feudal castle, Matsumae, built in 1606, has become a park. Next to it, the mouth of the Seikan Tunnel disgorges trains that have sped under the waves from Honshu.

On the Inland Sea, the town of Iwakuni is the site of the Kintai Bridge. Built in 1673, it was 600 feet (200 meters) long and was made entirely of fitted wood, with no nails. Floods swept the bridge away in 1950, but it has been rebuilt to the original design. Not far to the north, one of the three massive, concrete-and-metal land bridges built in the 1970s connects Honshu and Shikoku.

Close to the Kintai Bridge is the port of Hiroshima, one of Japan's major centers of shipping, manufacturing, and industry of all kinds. The tiny, peaceful island of Itsukushima in Hiroshima Bay is sacred to three sea goddesses and holds a Shinto shrine dating from 593 A.D. It is famous for the brilliant red *torii*, or arched Shinto gateway, that looks across the tidal waters of the bay to busy wharves and anchorages.

Hiroshima holds another sort of shrine as well: the skeleton of Japan's Industrial Exposition Hall, all that was left of the impressive building after the atomic bomb exploded above the center of the city on August 6, 1945. Not far away is a green and serene park called the Peace Memorial. It contains a brass bell that each visitor is asked to ring in memory of the bomb's victims. The park and an accompanying museum are now the site of many meetings and activities dedicated to world peace. The park's most moving monument lists the names of all the known bomb victims, with the epitaph "Repose in peace, for the error shall not be repeated."

The Japanese have always been good at borrowing elements from other cultures and changing them to suit their needs. They learned rice farming from the Koreans and are now the most productive farmers (in terms of crop yield per acre or hectare) in the world. They adapted Chinese writing and, later, English words to their own language. They learned how to make firearms from three shipwrecked mariners and grew into a formidable military power. And they applied American assembly-line techniques and business practices to their shattered postwar economy and became the second strongest economic force in the world.

Today, Japan faces the challenge of protecting its natural environment and its cultural heritage as it continues to develop its economy. Industry has made it powerful, but industry must be con-

Japanese men and women workers dine at a company cafeteria.

trolled or pollution will destroy much of what the Japanese love about their land. Similarly, Japan's trade policies have made the country rich, but now its partners are demanding equal trading rights. Japan must open its borders to freer trade if it is to remain on good terms with its world neighbors. As their country becomes more exposed to outside products and influences, many Japanese fear that imported Western music, clothing, and ideas may turn young people away from their own rich culture.

From earliest times until the late 19th century, Japan had little contact with the rest of the world. It took what it could use from other cultures but sent little of its own culture abroad. Now Japan is a significant world presence, striving to reconcile its new status with its old, carefully preserved traditions. If it succeeds in achieving this balance, it will become a true international leader, and the world will be greatly enriched.

‹G L O S S A R Y›

Amaterasu In Japanese mythology, Amaterasu is the sun goddess and the ancestor of the emperor's family.

Archipelago A chain of islands that are all part of the same undersea mountain formation.

Baiu Literally "plum rains," baiu refers to the seasonal rains that fall in late June and early July when the plums, or baiu, ripen on the trees.

Bakufu Literally "tent government" in Japanese. This refers to the form of government headed by the shoguns, who often ran the government from their field headquarters during their military campaigns.

Bunraku Japanese puppet theater, in which a narrator recites or sings the story while two or three large puppets act it out.

Bushido The samurai code of behavior that stressed honor, courage, loyalty, obedience, endurance, and military skill over book learning.

Caldera The basin formed by the hollow crater of a volcano. Many calderas (Spanish for "cauldron") fill with water and become lakes.

Chanoyu The traditional Japanese tea ceremony developed by courtiers, after tea became the national drink in the late 12th century. The chanoyu involved special utensils and ritual gestures that were supposed to express grace, refinement, courtesy, and discipline.

Hara-kiri	The ritual suicide by disembowelment with a special sword, through which a dishonored samurai could regain his good name.
Heiya	Small lowlands between the seacoast and the mountains that have become centers of agriculture and settlement over the centuries.
Hiragana	The standard Japanese alphabet of characters developed around 900 A.D. It is used today for most ordinary writing.
Ikebana	The art of flower arranging, developed by courtiers between the 8th and 13th centuries and still widely practiced today.
Joka-machi	These "castle towns" were the fortresses of feudal warlords that gradually grew into towns housing craftsmen, merchants, and workers.
Jomon	The name given to the earliest known Japanese civilization, from the word for "cord marks." The Jomon used to decorate their pottery with patterns made by cords tied in knots.
Juku	Schools where Japanese students prepare for the difficult entrance examinations for colleges and universities.
Kabuki	A form of traditional Japanese theater based on history or legend and featuring elaborate costumes and sets, music, and a narrator who chants the story while the actors perform.
Kago	A curtained stretcher or bed on which nobles were carried by men or animals.
Kami	Gods honored in the Shinto religion.
Kamikaze	The name given to the two typhoons, or "divine winds," that destroyed the invading Mongol fleets of Kublai Khan in the 13th century. Japanese "suicide squad" bomber pilots took the name during World War II.

Kanji   Written Chinese characters, introduced into Japan and adapted to the Japanese language around 400 A.D. About 1,850 of them are still used in Japanese.

Katakana   A Japanese alphabet developed around 800 A.D., whose characters are still used to write the names of foreign places and people.

Kuroshio   The Japan Current, sometimes called the Black Stream. It is a current of warm water that flows north from the central Pacific along the east coast of Japan.

Ronin   These "masterless samurai" were wandering mercenary soldiers who sometimes set up as highwaymen or bandits during Japan's feudal era.

Samurai   Warriors who developed out of the class of provincial government administrators and governors during the early part of the feudal period. The samurai became powerful and ruled the country through military leaders from the mid-12th through the mid-19th centuries.

Shogun   A military ruler. A series of shoguns ruled Japan from 1192 until the Meiji Restoration of 1868. Although the emperors were never dethroned, they had little or no real power while the shoguns controlled the military forces and the treasury.

Shogunate   The term used to describe the period of rule by a shogun or a particular family of shoguns.

Tenno   The title, which literally means "emperor of heaven," that was taken by a ruler of the Yamato family in the 5th century A.D.

Yayoi   An early Japanese culture that followed the Jomon, the Yayoi were named for the suburb of Tokyo where the first relics of their civilization were unearthed.

◄ I N D E X ►

ACKNOWLEDGMENTS

AP/Wide World Photos (pp. 66, 76, 90, 93, 94); Japanese Cultural Center (pp. 2, 22, 26, 50, 55, 57, 58a, 58b, 59a, 59b, 60a, 60b, 61, 62a, 62b, 63a, 63b, 64a, 64b, 71, 96, 98, 100, 103); Library of Congress (pp. 16, 18, 20, 24, 29, 32, 35 38, 42, 44, 46–47, 48, 52, 67, 69, 70, 72, 74, 78, 81, 84, 86, 88). Photo Research: Dixon & Turner Research Associates and Susan G. Holtz.

98/99 Garreth Stevens

W9-DET-290

NAVAL AVENUE ELEMENTARY SCHOOL

E
OPP

Oppenheim, Joanne

E
Opp

Could It Be?

NAVAL AVENUE ELEMENTARY SCHOOL

About The Bank Street Ready-to-Read Series

Seventy years of educational research and innovative teaching have given the Bank Street College of Education the reputation as America's most trusted name in early childhood education.

Because no two children are exactly alike in their development, we have designed the *Bank Street Ready-to-Read* series in three levels to accommodate the individual stages of reading readiness of children ages four through eight.

- ○ *Level 1:* GETTING READY TO READ—read-alouds for children who are taking their first steps toward reading.
- ● *Level 2:* READING TOGETHER—for children who are just beginning to read by themselves but may need a little help.
- ○ *Level 3:* I CAN READ IT MYSELF—for children who can read independently.

Our three levels make it easy to select the books most appropriate for a child's development and enable him or her to grow with the series step by step. The *Bank Street Ready-to-Read* books also overlap and reinforce each other, further encouraging the reading process.

We feel that making reading fun and enjoyable is the single most important thing that you can do to help children become good readers. And we hope you'll be a part of Bank Street's long tradition of learning through sharing.

The Bank Street College of Education

To Rory and Kraig
— J.O.

For a free color catalog describing Gareth Stevens' list of high-quality books and multimedia programs, call 1-800-542-2595 (USA) or 1-800-461-9120 (Canada). Gareth Stevens Publishing's Fax: (414) 225-0377.
See our catalog, too, on the World Wide Web: http://gsinc.com

Library of Congress Cataloging-in-Publication Data

Oppenheim, Joanne.
    Could it be? / by Joanne Oppenheim; illustrated by S. D. Schindler.
        p. cm. -- (Bank Street ready-to-read)
    Summary: Surrounded by the many sounds of spring, a hibernating bear is late in waking up, until he hears one very special sound.
        ISBN 0-8368-1770-2 (lib. bdg.)
        [1. Bears--Fiction. 2. Spring--Fiction. 3. Sound--Fiction.] I. Schindler, S. D., ill.
    II. Title. III. Series.
    PZ7.O616Co 1998
    [E]--dc21   97-47566

This edition first published in 1998 by
Gareth Stevens Publishing
1555 North RiverCenter Drive, Suite 201
Milwaukee, Wisconsin 53212 USA

© 1990 by Byron Preiss Visual Publications, Inc. Text © 1990 by Bank Street College of Education. Illustrations © 1990 by S. D. Schindler and Byron Preiss Visual Publications, Inc.

Published by arrangement with Bantam Doubleday Dell Books For Young Readers, a division of Bantam Doubleday Dell Publishing Group, Inc., New York, New York. All rights reserved.

Bank Street Ready To Read™ is a registered U.S. trademark of the Bank Street Group and Bantam Doubleday Dell Books For Young Readers, a division of Bantam Doubleday Dell Publishing Group, Inc.

All rights reserved. No part of this book may be reproduced, stored in a retrieval system, or transmitted in any form or by any means, electronic, mechanical, photocopying, or otherwise, without the prior written permission of the copyright holder.

Printed in Mexico

1 2 3 4 5 6 7 8 9 02 01 00 99 98

Bank Street Ready-to-Read™

Could It Be?

by Joanne Oppenheim
Illustrated by S. D. Schindler

A Byron Preiss Book

Gareth Stevens Publishing
MILWAUKEE

Once there was a big brown bear
who did not know it was spring.
He had been sleeping all winter long.
He did not hear the snow falling.
He did not hear the ice freezing.
He did not hear the wind howling.

He was sleeping snug and sound
in his den underground.

5

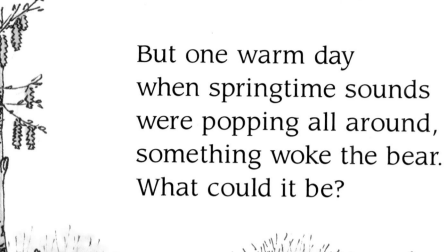

But one warm day
when springtime sounds
were popping all around,
something woke the bear.
What could it be?

Could it be the ice cracking
on the pond?
A fish heard that cracking sound.
But not the bear—
he was sleeping underground.

Could it be a bird singing?
A cat heard that singing sound.
But not the bear—
he was sleeping underground.

Could it be a cricket chirping
in the weeds?
A bunny heard that chirping sound.
But not the bear—
he was sleeping underground.

Could it be a frog croaking
on a log?
A duck heard that croaking sound.
But not the bear—
he was sleeping underground.

14

Could it be dewdrops dripping
from bursting buds?
A chipmunk heard that
drip-drop sound.

But not the bear—
he was sleeping underground.

NAVAL AVENUE ELEMENTARY SCHOOL

17

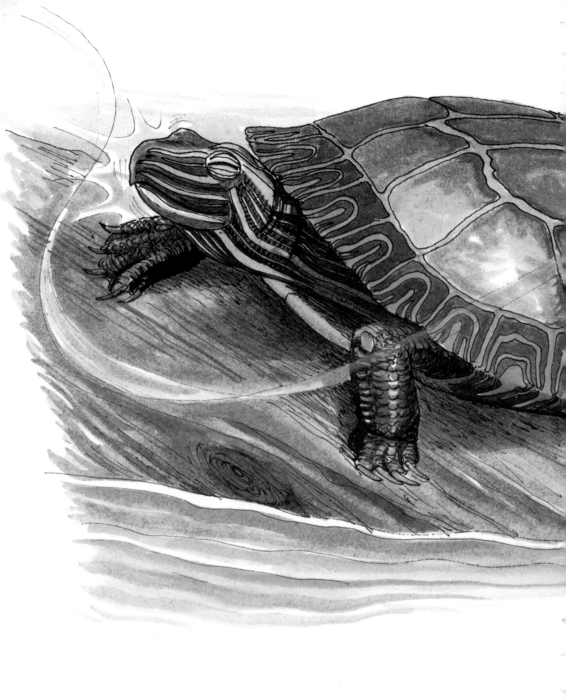

Could it be a turtle snapping?
A fly heard that snapping sound.
But not the bear—
he was sleeping underground.

Could it be raindrops pattering
on the leaves?
A deer heard that pattering sound.
But not the bear—
he was sleeping underground.

Could it be tulips popping?
A caterpillar creeping?
A butterfly fluttering?
A worm wiggling?
Grass growing?
Or even a rainbow shining?
Could anyone hear these things?
Could you?

But something woke the bear.
Listen—*z-z-z-z-z-z-z*.
Could it be a buzzing bee?
Z-z-z-z-z-z-z.
Yes, it was a bee,
a fuzzy buzzing bumblebee,
that woke the bear!

And the bear knew that
where there are bees,
there is honey!

26

So he followed the
buz-z-z-z-z-z-zing bee
into the springtime world
of singing birds,
chirping crickets,
croaking frogs,
dripping dewdrops,
and snapping turtles.

27

He followed the bee through
pattering raindrops,
past popping tulips,
creeping caterpillars,
fluttering butterflies,
wiggling worms, and
a shining rainbow . . .
until he found the honey.

And it was as sweet
as the sounds of spring!

31

Joanne Oppenheim is the author of more than two dozen picture books, including *Have You Seen Birds?*, which won the National Picture Book of the Year Award in Canada. A former elementary school teacher, she is co-author of *Choosing Books for Kids* and is currently a Senior Editor for the Bank Street College Media Group. Ms. Oppenheim divides her time between New York City and her home in Monticello, New York.

S. D. Schindler has had a lifelong fascination with plants and animals. Studying nature is one of his favorite pasttimes. *Could It Be?* is one of numerous books relating to nature for which he has done illustrations. Others include the *Creepy Crawly Book* and *My First Bird Book,* which he also wrote. Mr. Schindler studied biology at the University of Pennsylvania and currently lives on three acres of woods in Philadelphia.

NAVAL AVENUE ELEMENTARY SCHOOL